Beyond the edge of the empire – Caledonians, Picts and Romans

Fraser Hunter

ISBN 978-0-9540999-2-3

Fraser Hunter, BSc, PhD, FSA Scot, FSA

Fraser Hunter trained in Archaeological Sciences at Bradford University from 1987-1991,
and was then appointed Iron Age and Roman curator at the National Museums of
Scotland, a post he still holds. In 2004 he completed a part-time PhD from Bradford
University on the evidence for the carnyx, an animal-headed trumpet, from across Iron
Age Europe, which is currently being prepared for publication. He has an active field-
work programme, with major excavations at the findspot of the carnyx from Deskford
(Moray), on the hillfort of Traprain Law (East Lothian), and on the Iron Age settlement
at Birnie (Moray), which is detailed in this book.

The question of the impact of Rome on the indigenous peoples of Scotland and elsewhere
is a topic which he finds fascinating, and much of his research is geared to this. Other
areas of active research include Iron Age metalwork and Celtic art.

Printed by A4 Design & Print Ltd, Inverness

Contents

The Birnie bird mount (length 21 mm).

Introduction

The Picts are an endlessly discussed subject. Their placenames, their art, their settlements and their language have been scrutinised by a wide range of scholars, as previous lectures in this series demonstrate. Yet the thrust of this work has been on what may be termed the classic Pictish period, the sixth-ninth centuries AD when the distinctive Pictish art styles flourished. Although our earliest references to people termed Picts date to the late third century AD, there has been surprisingly little detailed work on these early centuries. They fall between the normal disciplinary boundary of prehistorians and early historians: studies of the Iron Age 'proper' typically stop in the early centuries AD (e.g. Hingley 1992; Armit 1997a), with later scholars picking up the story in the post-Roman period, after AD 400 (e.g. Alcock 2003; Laing 1975; Foster 2004; an exception is Smyth 1989). Despite pleas for a 'long Iron Age' on Scandinavian lines spanning most of the first millennia (e.g. Armit 1990b, 1-2; Foster 1990; Harding 2004), most scholars have stuck to traditional perspectives. Yet this limbo period of the third and fourth centuries AD is a crucial one in understanding how the societies of the Iron Age transformed into those of the Early Historic period.

In this quest, the presence and proximity of the Roman empire in the first four centuries AD is crucial. Although there was little permanent occupation north of the Forth, the influence of Rome stretched far beyond the formal frontier. Indeed it is widely suggested that Rome inadvertently created the Picts; it was the proximity and threat of Rome which led the disparate Iron Age tribes north of the Forth to amalgamate into larger, more centrally controlled groups which ultimately posed a serious military threat to Rome. This theory, developed by John Mann (1974), has been a highly influential one. It is based on the (rather limited) literary sources and analogy to events on the Continent; essentially, that there are fewer tribal names recorded in the later period than the earlier. My purpose here is to reconsider the impact of Rome on the peoples north of the Forth in the first four centuries AD, from an archaeological perspective, to look at the uses these groups made of Rome, and to consider anew the various theories about the effect of Rome. While I will look at a range of sources of evidence, my focus will be on the finds of Roman objects from non-Roman sites.

For almost four centuries Scotland north of the Forth was on the edge of a mighty empire. At times relations were hostile, and a series of invasions and incursions in both directions are recorded in the historical sources (Maxwell 1987, 43). Yet these sources are few in number and one-sided in perspective. Conflict was only one of the relationships between Rome and her northern neighbours: we would expect to see trade, diplomacy, tribute and so on, but these are barely hinted at in the history books. It is too easy to take the Roman perspective because they have a voice: the sources record the Roman views of conquest and occupation in this far-off world, of threats to frontier security and civilised life from these northern barbarians. Yet we must also consider the local perspective: Rome was a fact of life, not purely a threat, and there were opportunities to be had. Rome, wittingly or unwittingly, played a role within indigenous societies. What uses were made of this, and how did they change? What effect did this proximity have on local society? These are some of the themes to be tackled here.

Models

The effects of Rome have been studied by a number of scholars, with very divergent views. We may identify four main models.

Minimal impact. The presence of Rome was but a hiccup in the development of Iron Age societies in Scotland which had no lasting impact (e.g. Hanson 2003, 216; Keppie 1989, 72-73; Harding 2004, 179-199, 203). This may be termed the nativist perspective. It would make Scotland more or less unique around the edges of the Roman empire; elsewhere there is plentiful evidence that the presence and proximity of Rome had a considerable impact at some distance from the frontier (e.g. Jørgensen et al 2003; Wells 1999).

Amalgamation. As outlined above, this sees Rome as a catalyst which led smaller social units to amalgamate into larger ones, capable of dealing with the empire on more level terms (Mann 1974). This has parallels in free Germany, with the emergence of larger political units beyond the frontier (e.g. Heather 1994).

Power source. This sees Rome being used locally as a resource to draw on within local power politics. It has been proposed at two periods. In the first and second centuries AD it is suggested that control of access to Roman goods was an important source of power and prestige within local society (e.g. Macinnes 1984). For the later and post-Roman periods, Rome has been seen as a source of inspiration to emulate or hark back to (e.g. Smyth 1989, 16-18; Laing & Laing 1984, 269-273). This has mainly been argued for southern Scotland, but it has also been suggested for the phenomenon of Pictish art (Laing & Laing 1984); this latter point will be explored more thoroughly later.

Destabilise. This is linked to the previous theory. Rome's impact has been seen as a bad one, with societies becoming too reliant on Roman goods or markets as a crucial part of social interaction: the upper echelons of society became dependent on Roman exotica to display their power and circulate as gifts to lubricate social relations. When they were not as readily available in the post-Antonine period this had a destabilising effect, with social change and possibly collapse (Macinnes 1984, 244-245; Hill 1982a, 8-12; Armit 1999). In this model, rather than *pax Romana*, Rome had a highly negative effect, even if unintentionally. This too has mainly been argued for southern Scotland, although Armit (1999) has developed a related theory for the souterrain settlements of Angus, Perthshire and Fife: he sees these as expanding to accommodate the supply needs of the Roman army in the Antonine period, and collapsing when this was withdrawn. North-east Scottish palynological evidence has also been interpreted as showing negative effects (Whittington and Edwards 1993), although the dataset is as yet small; there are too few securely-dated pollen samples from the area to attempt any synthetic treatment (Tipping 1994, illus 2).

It is clear from this that there is no consensus about the effect of Rome. Indeed, while a diversity of interpretation is a sign of a healthy discipline, it is worrying that such widely divergent views can be expressed in the literature with little or no debate about their relative merits – they seem to be matters of belief rather than analysis. It is hoped that what follows will go some way to stirring such debate.

Caledonians and Picts – who, what and where?

First we should consider terminology. In my title I use the terms 'Caledonian' and 'Pict'. Both are historical terms which are awkward to correlate with archaeological evidence. Much ink has been spilt over definitions of people, place and period: who were the Caledonians and Picts, where were they and when were they? I do not propose to get embroiled in the detail of this essentially historical argument, but would like to make a few points to clarify my own position for what follows.

A brief history
The history of Roman Scotland is dealt with in detail by others (e.g. Breeze 1982; Frere 1991), but it is worth reiterating the key aspects of the historical sources for the political geography of Iron Age Scotland. There are minimal records before the Flavian invasions, but with these first substantial incursions historical sources stutter into life, the key ones being Tacitus' *Agricola*, frustratingly short on geographical and political details, and Ptolemy's *Geographia* (a second century source drawing on Flavian material) which has carried with it enough uncertainties to fuel generations of scholarship. These sources have recently been interrogated to good effect by Fraser (2005), with

valuable insights into political units in Iron Age Scotland which will be considered further below. The sources for the second century are poorer; there are indications of troubles during Hadrian's reign (e.g. Breeze 2003) and scanty references to the brief Antonine occupation. Historical evidence remains difficult to interpret for the later second century, but there are recurrent suggestions of troubles in the north. These become clearer in the run-up to the Severan invasions of AD 208-211, when the Caledonians and Maeatae are named and shamed as the troublesome tribes which required imperial intervention. While the much-vaunted victories proclaimed in propaganda coins and sculpture appear to be more political spin than reality, the frontier remained quiet (at least in literary terms) until the early fourth century, when the first conflict with the Picts is recorded. Thereafter references are scattered thinly across the histories of the fourth and early fifth centuries, as noted above (Maxwell 1987, 43).

The depth of feeling about the Picts within the Roman world is reflected by a find from the Rhine frontier which has been curiously under-studied in a Scottish context. This is a dice tower found on the Roman rural settlement of Vettweiß-Froitzheim, behind the lower German *limes* near Cologne (fig 1; Horn 1989; Hartley et al 2006, 135; Keppie 1989, 71). It is made of copper alloy sheets with an opening at the base of one face leading to a series of steps: dice were thrown in the top and rolled down the steps. Openwork decoration covers the sides, with the inscription 'VTERE FELIX VIVAS' (Good luck, live well) running round three sides. The front bears a longer inscription covering its whole face: 'PICTOS VICTOS HOSTIS DELETA LVDITE SECVRI' – 'the Picts are beaten, the enemy annihilated, let us play without a care'. This six-line-six-letter format is well-known from gaming contexts, connected to the dice-game *ludus duodecim scriptorum*, a race game similar to backgammon (Murray 1951, 30-31). Unfortunately the piece is not from a closed context, but a fourth century date seems assured from the decorative style. Clearly the concept of the Picts was alive in popular as well as literary culture, at least on the neighbouring frontier.

Naming the peoples

This brief review emphasises that both 'Caledonian' and 'Pict' come down to us from external sources; they were recorded not by the people themselves but by the Romans. With Caledonians, there is good evidence that this was also a term in use in the Iron Age by these people and their neighbours: it is preserved in placenames in the Atholl area of Perthshire (Dunkeld, Schiehallion and Rohallion; Watson 1926, 21-22), while within Roman Britain, in Colchester, one Lossio Veda had himself described on an inscription as '*nepos Vepogeni Caledo*' – grandson of Vepogenus (or of Vepo born), a Caledonian (RIB I, 191; Koch 1980, 89). It seems then that Caledonian was a genuine local term. The

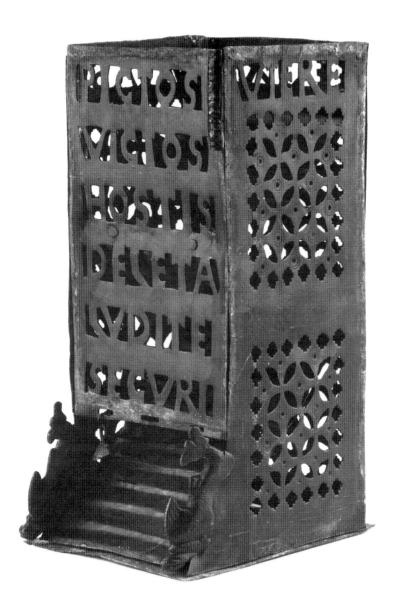

Fig 1 *Dice tower from Vettweiß-Froitzheim, Germany.*
© *Rheinishes Landesmuseum Bonn.*

same cannot be said for Pict: although the derivation is much debated, it is most probably a Roman slang word for 'painted people' (Anderson 1987, 7; Smyth 1989, 44) with the same origins as the word for Britons, *Pretani* (Watson 1926, 13; Cunliffe 2001, 94-95). The term may have stuck because once written down in Roman sources it acquired an authority, and became fact for subsequent (external) commentators. Yet, while not a term used by the Picts themselves at this time, it did have a popular currency in the Roman world beyond the literary sources, as the German dice tower indicates.

Yet, although 'Picts' are not mentioned until the late third century, there is no simple sequence of Caledonians being succeeded in the sources by Picts. The problem with both 'Caledonian' and 'Pict' is that Roman authors were very variable in their usage. The former described both people and place, the latter just a people, but both were used very imprecisely and it is arguably more realistic to see them as general shorthand for 'north British barbarians' rather than seeking any greater detail in their meaning. Caledonia was very much used as a literary device for the land beyond the Forth (or occasionally for all of northern Britain). Caledonians were variously a tribe, a confederacy, and part of the Picts.[1] The term Caledonia remained in use as a geographical term (or personification) into the late Roman period (e.g. by Claudian in 396-400; Miller 1975), but the recorded tribal names change, as charted by Mann (1974). His preferred sequence is outlined in fig 2, which he saw as reflecting the gradual amalgamation of smaller units into larger ones. However, with such sparse data other interpretations are possible; for instance, Anderson (1987, 7) considers the Dicalydones and Verturiones as two of potentially several units rather than the only two subdivisions of the Picts, while Maxwell (1987, 32) points to a persistent bipartite division either side of the Mounth long before the Picts. Earlier tribal names also persist into the Pictish period: the Verturiones survive much later in *Fortriu*, while the Maeatae, who should have been absorbed into this wider consortium, inconveniently persist as the *Miathi* into the sixth century (Watson 1926, 20, 57-59, 68-69; Smyth 1989, 43; Alcock 2003, 42). The unity of the Picts can be over-emphasised; there is considerable evidence for much smaller political units in the Pictish area, not dissimilar in scale to those listed by Ptolemy.

The problems may be as much of our own making as that of our sources. We expect named groups to inhabit our protohistory, and latch onto the sparse sources like terriers. Yet we must be wary of both the biases in our sources and the nature of Iron Age societies. Our tribal geography of early Scotland relies heavily on Ptolemy. Many of the 'tribal names' are attested only in his *Geography*, or in derivatives such as the *Ravenna Cosmography* (Rivet & Smith 1979, 193-194); as noted, other writers confirm some names (such as the Caledonii) and add others (Boresti, Maeatae, and so forth). Some of the tribes recorded by classical writers

Fig 2 *Reconstruction of the sequence of tribes recorded in Scotland by Classical authors (from Breeze 1982, figs 1, 28 & 39). (a) Late first century; (b) early third century; (c) fourth century.*

never reappear in later historical sources, but others do seem to become fixtures of the local political scene in the following centuries. Early Historic sources record the Verturiones and the Maeatae, as noted, while forms of the Votadini, and less certainly the Damnonii, Novantae and Venicones, occur (Rivet & Smith 1979, 508-509; Jackson 1969, 5; Fraser 2005, 34, 36, 141 n.42; Watson 1926, 27; Koch 1980). Others have a toponymic trace which suggests some longevity: the Smertae, for instance, are probably commemorated in Carn Smeart in Sutherland (Watson 1926, 17). It seems these tribes were not entirely Roman inventions although, as discussed below, it is unclear what they represent. However, the problems of these accounts are clear. Some areas seem over-inhabited with names, others seriously under-populated, while the available sources rarely agree. The classic example of these problems is the Boresti (if they are even a tribe), named by Tacitus (*Agricola* 38, 3) but otherwise unknown. The same is true of the *Anavionenses*,[2] too readily swept by previous scholars into the supposed Brigantian confederacy, but in truth more likely to reflect a valley-based unit, more consistent with the smaller-scale societies suggested for the British Iron Age (Birley 2001).

This fluidity should not surprise us. The earliest recorded political units are frequently characterised by instability, symptomatic of societies developing into complex forms. This is seen notably in the sources for the conquest of southern Britain: Caesar mentions tribes he encountered in his invasion of 54 BC which did not survive to be named at the time of the Claudian invasion (Birley 2001, 17; Cunliffe 2005, 139). Equally, the coinages of southern England record individuals, presumed to be kings or elite leaders, most of whom are otherwise unknown (Allen 1944). Attempts to write history from this are unprovable, but the fluidity of the political scene reflected by changing names and varying areas of influence seen in coin distributions indicates the inherent fluidity of these early power-units. This is not surprising, as these early attempts at politically-larger units are characterised elsewhere in Europe by both instability and a marked tendency to create new identities to fit new situations (e.g. Carroll 2002, 107-109; Woolf 1998; Roymans 2004).

The problem is compounded by Roman approaches to barbarian groups. Some authors (notably Caesar, *de Bello Gallico* and Tacitus, *Germania*) present detailed ethnographies, but there is also a recurring trend in Roman characterisations of barbarian tribes as big groups, equivalent to nation states, who could thus be portrayed as a worthwhile enemy. This is seen clearly in the propaganda portrayal of defeated enemies in coins and sculpture: the units are Germans or Gauls, not Chatti, Cherusci, Aedui and so on. This in turn created the vision of large-scale ethnic units of protohistory which remain embedded in our study today, such as Celts, Gauls and Germans.

There is a further problem in understanding the nature of even the smaller tribal units. How did a 'tribe' such as the Novantae or the Votadini work? They are painted across substantial landscape areas by Ptolemy, but archaeology provides little evidence of such paramount chiefs controlling large areas. Are these unstable alliances, captured in Roman snapshots, held together by the politics, threat or charisma of individuals? Are we seeing a pattern of elite self-identity, affiliations at an upper social echelon with little meaning to the masses? Or are these genuine expressions of regional self-identity, patterns of contact forged across generations? Archaeologists have shown little taste in recent years to tackle the difficult issue of regionality and its social reality, but this is crucial to any attempt at understanding our sparse protohistory.

I do not wish to get further bogged down in this treacherous terrain, but this discussion has highlighted something of the complexity and biases of the historical evidence. Neat though Mann's theory is, it is not unequivocally supported by the historical sources. While the process of political coalescence in the face of Rome is well-documented by a combination of sources elsewhere beyond the frontier (notably in Germany; Heather 1994), in Scotland we must seek archaeological evidence to support changes at this time before accepting the theory.

How then should we use the terms Caledonian and Pict? Some scholars stick to the historical chronology, with AD 297 as the boundary, while accepting that the Picts were not incomers and therefore terming what went before 'proto-Pict' (Wainwright 1956, 15; Harding 2004, 248-249). I share others' discomfort at this term (Ritchie 1984, 1-2; Ralston 1987, 15), not least because it implies these earlier peoples are simply part of a natural evolution towards the Picts rather than being worthy of study in their own right. Other authors advocate back-projecting the term 'Picts' to the first century AD (Smyth 1989, 43-53), but I do not see this colonisation of the Iron Age as a useful process; and why stop arbitrarily at the first century? This speaks of a historian's agenda rather than an archaeologist's. Here the historical sources shall be taken at what seems close to face value, with Caledonians predominating as a term until the late third century and Picts thereafter. In the terminology advocated below, the Caledonians fall into the early and middle Roman Iron Age (to c. AD 250) and the Picts occupy the late Roman Iron Age onwards (AD 250-400+).

A key question to arise from this is the link between archaeology and history. Do the changing names reflect real changes? In other words, without the historical sources would we identify any change? Did society in Scotland change dramatically in this period, and if so what role did Rome have? It is this question which will dominate the rest of this essay.

Roman finds and Iron Age society

Evidence and problems
The main evidence used here is the presence of Roman finds on non-Roman sites – the material witness of contact between the peoples. These have been catalogued by several scholars (Curle 1932; Robertson 1970; Robertson 1983; Hunter 2001), and provide a rich resource – but one with a number of health warnings. The key one is their condition. Unlike the wealthy objects known from burials and hoards beyond the German frontier (Eggers 1951; Lund Hansen 1987), the vast majority of Scottish finds derive from settlement sites, and as a result are fragmentary and worn. This is a poor reflection of their original condition, but too often commentators have failed to see past this basic taphonomic issue (Hunter 2002). A worn sherd of samian was once a grand decorated bowl, fit to grace a Roman officer's table; tiny sherds of glass vessels were once spectacular and rare drinking vessels (fig 3). Their present condition belies their past significance.

BURIAL   **SETTLEMENT**

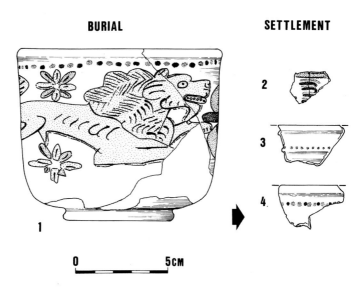

0 _____ 5CM

***Fig 3** The problem of fragmentary finds. The intact painted cup from a burial at Jesendorf, Germany (1; from Voß 1998, taf 37 & 56) gives an idea of how the unimpressive Scottish fragments would once have looked. The Scottish finds are from settlements at Traprain Law, East Lothian (2; Curle 1915, 108; NMS GV 41); Dunollie, Argyll (3; from Alcock & Alcock 1987, ill 9); and Clickhimin, Shetland (4; from Hamilton 1968, fig 62). Drawn by Alan Braby.*

A second key problem is the debate over when these items came to Scotland. Some scholars have argued that much of this material arrived after the end of Roman Britain, and circulated in fragmentary form as curios or talismans in Early Historic society.[3] It is easy to see how this view arose; much of the material is fragmentary and many of the sites saw occupation in the Early Historic period as well. However, I do not think this Early Historic 'reliquary' scenario was the dominant process, nor even a major distorter. There are plenty of instances of sherds from the same vessel on a site, implying it arrived intact rather than as a reliquary sherd (e.g. Fairy Knowe, Stirlingshire and Castlehill, Ayrshire; Willis 1998a; Smith 1919, 127). Equally, the strong selectivity in types of pottery, which Alcock (note 3) interpreted as the selection of colourful sherds for the secondary relic-trade, is better explained as a deliberate selection of certain preferred types of (intact) fine tablewares, as discussed below. Finally, large-scale excavation has regularly shown that many of these Early Historic sites had Roman Iron Age precursors (as at Dunadd and Buiston; Lane & Campbell 2000; Crone 2000). It is thus unsurprising that residual material occurs in later layers, a common phenomenon on long-lived sites; we may note the third century BC brooch from the Howe, Orkney, found in layers of seventh-ninth century AD date (Ballin Smith 1994, 223-224).

Of course it is impossible to be sure of any individual object's life history, and post-Roman use of Roman objects is also well-attested. Often this involved spectacular items, as in the crystal reused for the Anglo-Saxon 'Alfred Jewel' (Kornbluth 1989); intaglios and cameos were set in the great medieval reliquaries, such as the shrine of the Magi in Köln or the Lothar Cross in Aachen (Zwierlein-Diehl 1998; Grimme 1968, Taf 3-4), or reused as seals, as perhaps with the intaglio lost in the medieval abbey sewer at Paisley (Malden 2000, fig 8; more generally Henig 1978, 159-164; Henig 2000). More mundane objects could also have an afterlife: this is seen best with samian, such as sherds bearing Saxon graffiti at London and Worcester (Wallace 2006; Wheeler 1935, 194, pl XXI; Dalwood et al 1992, 125, fig 2). However, such reuse is a rarity; for most of the Scottish material, the arguments rehearsed above suggest there is no reason to argue for post-Roman arrival in the country. The bulk of this material most plausibly arrived intact in Scotland during the Roman period. This is not to deny that it could have a long life afterwards: if these objects were valued items, they could have been curated for centuries and circulated widely within local society, ending up far from where they left Roman hands. There are good examples of this from Iron Age burials in Scandinavia, where the date of the burial is several centuries younger than some of the objects with it (Nielsen 1988, 152-155; Helander 1997). Scotland lacks such a burial tradition to freeze an object's history, but the evidence of repair and reuse on many Roman items points to an extended life, although the length of this is uncertain (e.g. the removal of vessel bases for reuse as small cups at Fairy Knowe, the repair of a samian mortarium at Okstrow, or the reuse of samian sherds as polishers at many sites; Willis 1998a, 330-331; Curle 1932, 395; Robertson 1970, 208).

The final issue is the problem of much later intrusive material, such as souvenirs of the Grand Tour or, more commonly, of wartime service in North Africa. This has led to large numbers of late Roman coins, minted in the eastern Empire, turning up in Scotland. A study of their mint-marks by Casey (1984) showed that few were genuine ancient losses, and at present this whole category of material has to be dismissed (although see Robertson 1993). There will be a residue of genuine ancient losses within this, but the detailed audit combining find circumstances and information from the coins themselves has not been carried out. Because of this, stray coin finds will not be considered here in any detail.

Interpreting the evidence
This leaves us with an extensive dataset for analysis: over 200 Iron Age sites with Roman finds, around 40 votive or burial sites, and over 100 stray finds (fig 4). The scale of this is not often realised; Roman finds were widespread in Iron Age Scotland. Recent excavations and metal-detecting finds have greatly increased our knowledge of the stray finds in particular: for instance, since Robertson's (1970) work there has been a doubling in known Roman findspots (excluding coins) in Moray and a four-fold increase in Fife. On settlement sites, assessment of a sample of southern Scottish Iron Age sites shows that Roman finds occur on 40% of them (unpublished work by writer); as this amalgamates pre- and post-RIA sites, the contemporary abundance must have been considerably greater. There is regional variety within this: a similar exercise for excavated Orcadian brochs shows that only c.25% have produced Roman finds. However, it is clear that in many areas Roman finds are far from rare. Given their relative abundance we cannot identify them simply as 'status' items but need more complex explanations.

The analysis below concentrates largely on site finds, burials and hoards. Stray finds are only considered for the period after c. AD 160, when they are much less likely to result from Roman activity. This dataset has been analysed previously to look for patterns in the occurrence of Roman finds on Iron Age sites (Hunter 2001); here only a summary will be given. The sites with Roman finds are split more or less evenly north and south of the Antonine Wall. However, making detailed comparisons between sites is difficult because they have been excavated at different times and scales to different standards by different people. Some (such as Traprain Law in East Lothian) have produced hundreds of fragments, but most have only one or two scraps. Yet the scraps are significant, as argued above, since they are the surviving residues of important

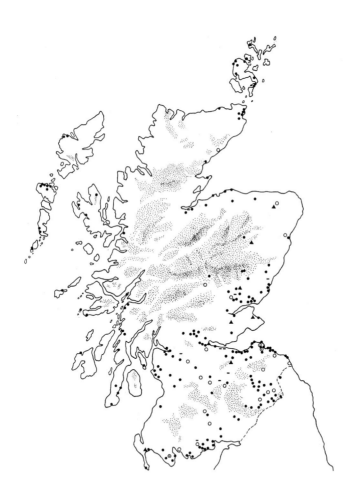

Fig 4 *Distribution of Roman finds on non-Roman sites in Scotland (as known to the author, June 2006). Key: solid dots = settlement finds; open circles = hoards (excluding coins); dots in circles = both settlement and hoard; triangles = burials; dash = uncertain. Stray finds are not plotted. Drawn by Marion O'Neil.*

objects. To try to get round this problem we can consider the range of finds rather than absolute numbers, following approaches pioneered by Steven Willis (e.g. Willis 1997; 1998b) – the presence or absence of categories such as samian, glass, brooches and so on for each site. This gives a picture of the range of Roman material available to its inhabitants. Thus, even on a site which has only seen small-scale excavation, the range of finds gives some indication of the

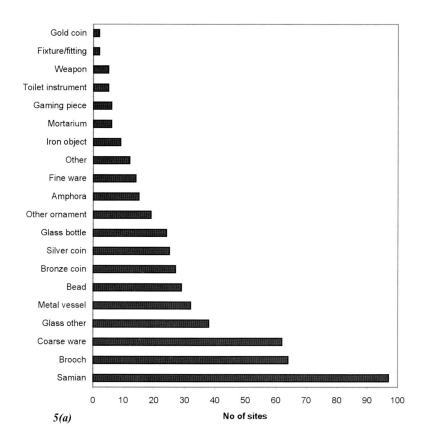

5(a)

Fig 5 *Selective adoption of Roman goods in Iron Age societies (using data known to the author as of June 2006). (a) Different categories of objects, ranked according to the number of sites where they occur. (b) Comparison of the frequency of key categories north and south of the Antonine Wall. Note that the number of metal vessels is high in fig 5a because hoards are included as well as site finds; for a caveat about the interpretation of such hoards, see Hunter (1997, 117-8).*

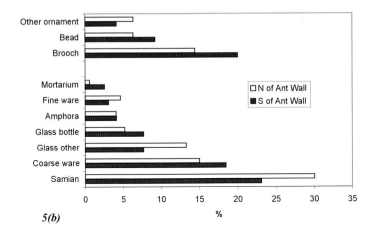

5(b)

original assemblage. Of course a single sherd from a small trial trench is still unlikely to be representative of the original 'find population' of the site, and this approach also makes no distinctions for varying quantities of material, but it provides a first-level correction for excavation bias.

Choosy natives – selective adoption of Roman material culture
It is immediately clear from the limited range of Roman finds found on Iron Age sites, that there was a strong selection process in what was adopted (fig 5). There is a marked lack of everyday tools and coarse pottery, with a focus instead on two areas: jewellery and items connected with eating and drinking. The bulk of the jewellery is brooches, though there is a much smaller quantity of beads, bangles and finger rings. The focus on food is emphasised not just by the quantity of eating and drinking vessels but by their type. Samian tableware dominates over mundane coarse wares, in contrast to a typical Roman fort where coarse wares were the predominant cooking, storing and serving vessels. Recent study of the glass by Dominic Ingemark (2003) has shown that this too is selective, with a high percentage of vessels connected with the serving and drinking of alcohol; even more strikingly, he notes a strong preference for rare types such as painted cups and pillar-moulded bowls. There is also a series of bronze vessels from wine services, known as occasional fragments from site finds but more often from hoards (Hunter 1997, 117-118).

These habits of flashy jewellery and feasting were very much an existing part of Iron Age life: the ornate metalwork of the period is dominated by jewellery and cauldrons, along with weaponry and horse harness, illustrating the pleasures of the local elites (MacGregor 1976). This suggests Roman material was adopted into Iron Age habits rather than causing any major change. There was an existing openness to exotica, especially in southern Scotland (Hunter 1997, 121), and Roman finds could be fitted readily into that.

Having said that, there were clearly changes. The jewellery was rather different in concept from that used locally. While indigenous fashion involved a range of smaller personal ornaments such as bangles and bead necklaces, brooches were all but unknown: pins were the main means of fastening clothing. The wearing of the safety-pin style of brooch was an alien idea, an innovation, and the adoption of this new ornament type was itself a selective one, apparently following two principles. One was a fondness for brooches at the ornate end of the spectrum, such as the heavily-enamelled examples from Carlungie and Birnie (Wainwright 1953, Plate XVI; Appendix 3; fig 6). The other was for brooches which in form or decoration reflected local taste, for instance in the use of trumpet motifs and enamelling (see Hunter 1996, 122-123 for further discussion). The Roman brooches thus represent an adaptation and development of local ornamental habits to new circumstances. These brooches were also relatively small and subtle, and thus only truly visible at close range.[4] Only those who got close to the wearer could appreciate them, and thus they functioned in an environment where close interpersonal contact was the main social forum – the conversation rather than the public spectacle.

The feasting and drinking equipment also represents a change from local practices: as Ian Ralston has pointed out (pers comm), it suggests the dinner party rather than the feast. In contrast to the more communal scale of consumption represented by massive indigenous cauldrons, Roman tablewares were adapted for smaller-scale dining using smaller and more personal vessels. Such personal tableware was all but absent in the local Iron Age: pottery was predominantly large bucket-like vessels, and other media such as wood are also dominated by large containers.[5] Of course we cannot know how the Roman vessels were being used. Jeff Davies has suggested that the popularity of large decorated samian bowls (Dr 37 type) on Welsh native sites reflects their use as communal bowls to be passed round the assembled throng (Arnold & Davies 2000, 112); the Scottish evidence has not been considered in this light.[6] Yet such bowls are markedly smaller than what went before and suggest small social gatherings. This hints at a change in social interactions, from the large-scale feast for clients, kin and competitors to a more 'invitation-only' elite group. The feasting culture probably continued concurrently with this, as cauldrons are certainly known from the Roman Iron Age (e.g. Piggott 1953, fig 7), but as with the brooches it seems there was a more personal level of interaction among some restricted groups of society.

Fig 6 *Ornate Roman brooches from Birnie. © National Museums of Scotland.*

What was being consumed at these elite soirées? It is possible that the habit of wine-drinking was adopted (Ingemark 2003 & forthcoming), although in contrast to contact-phase Gaul and southern England, when rich sites were awash with wine amphorae, there are very few on Scottish Iron Age sites. Of the few examples (c.15 sites), the vast bulk are Dressel 20 olive oil amphorae, arguably reused to carry other materials. Only one wine amphora is known so far, from Carlungie, Angus (of Gauloise 12 type; Wainwright 1963, 147; Fitzpatrick 2003, 63). This was a small, portable vessel; many sherds survived, indicating it arrived on site intact. In general, if wine was being consumed, it has left little trace in the ceramics. However, the problem may be one of container visibility: an amphora is a sensible solution to the problem of moving wine by ship, but a poor option when that transport moves to pack-animal.

Getting hold of the goods - selective access to Roman finds
We can also consider the range of Roman goods arriving on any particular site. By counting the number of categories (brooches, coarse ware, glass and so forth) we have an index which separates sites receiving a broad range of finds from others with more limited access. This can be interpreted in social terms as reflecting a hierarchy of access; powerful sites with lots of finds, less important sites with fewer (see Hunter 2001 for full discussion).

These access patterns show strong regional variations. The south-east reveals a very marked hierarchy, with a few very rich sites, a clear 'middle tier' of rich sites, and the bulk with only one or two find-types. This suggests a strong social control over access, with the Roman objects coming into central sites (such as Traprain Law) and being redistributed from there, presumably via existing social networks, bonds of kin and clientage. This was less marked in the south-west where no very rich sites are so far known, suggesting smaller-scale power structures.[7] North of the Forth was different again: the area from Forth to Tay has revealed a number of rich sites, notably lowland brochs such as Hurly Hawkin (Angus) or Fairy Knowe (Stirlingshire), and looks similar socially to the south-east. However, north of the Mounth, in Aberdeenshire and the Moray Firth, there was much less clear differentiation between sites, with most having a limited range. This suggests a much more locally-based social system, without people or groups controlling great tracts of land (a topic discussed in more detail later). The Atlantic zone similarly lacks strong evidence of hierarchies. Here, furthest from the frontier, Roman finds are markedly rarer. This is not to suggest that they were less valued here – indeed, as even rarer items they may have been more sought after. There does seem to have been greater selectivity further north, with the emphasis increasingly on quality rather than quantity (Hunter 2001, 298-300).

This analysis suggests that Roman items had a real social value throughout Iron Age Scotland. They were readily if selectively adopted as markers of identity and status, reinforcing bonds between people as the objects moved around within Iron Age society. Differences between sites and areas give us valuable clues to the nature of the societies in different parts of the country, but in all cases it can be argued that Roman objects were seen as desirable commodities.

Change through time

A drawback with this analysis of Roman goods coming onto Iron Age sites is that it bundles all the Roman material, spanning some 400 years of contact, into a single picture. In part this is the result of the limited quantity of data and the difficulties in getting detailed chronologies for many finds. However, it is clear that there were changes through time which merit more detailed attention.

There have been attempts to look at the differences between first and second century material (Macinnes 1989), but these are hindered by difficulties in dating. The production date of certain classes, such as coins and fine-ware pottery, is well known, and this has been taken to reflect more general chronological patterns of contact. However, the use of such material could well have been lengthy: we can date production, but rarely know the length of its use-life. Much metalwork and glass can only be given a broad late first-second century bracket; other material which could be more closely dated and might be expected to have a shorter life-cycle, such as coarse pottery, has received little specialist attention. Another problem is changing chronological patterns of availability, which reflect wider economic trends within Roman Britain rather than anything specifically due to connections with Scotland. This has been demonstrated most clearly for pottery, where Going (1992) has noted variations in pottery production, with periods where pot was rarer and thus earlier forms were likely to persist in use. Worryingly for Scotland, two of the peak production periods (and thus periods whose wares are likely to persist) broadly correlate with the Flavian and Antonine periods. Thus the chronological patterns have to be treated with caution, as certain periods will be inherently under-represented. Given this, we should be wary of arguing for detailed chronological correlations, for instance with periods of military occupation (contra Erdrich et al 2000, 451-452). This is unfortunate, as for the south of Scotland this affects whether the area was within or beyond the Roman province. At the moment, it is difficult to approach such subtleties.

In this essay a four-fold division of the Roman Iron Age is proposed (table 1). The rationale behind this is as follows. The vast bulk of finds from the Roman period fall into the Flavian and Antonine periods (here the early Roman Iron Age: ERIA), but while certain categories (such as coins and much pot) can be dated more closely, others cannot. The idea behind this division is that items with a broad dating range are accommodated within the ERIA on the balance of probability, with only the more distinctive material being classified to the other periods. The late Roman division is a relatively simple one. By around 250 many finds classes had changed: many brooch types (such as trumpets and headstuds) went out of production in the late second / early third century, as did samian (e.g. Tyers 1996, fig 91), new glass types developed from the later third century, while 238 marked the final demise of the *denarius*, the silver coin which had been the mainstay of the Roman currency since the Republic. It is thus a useful broad watershed. Some finds are trickier to categorise: for instance some brooch types start before 75 or run after 160, but if the bulk of their accepted production span lies within the ERIA then they are placed there in this analysis. The aim is to identify material whose production certainly or most probably does not date to the main periods of direct Roman occupation of the country. As such it may classify some finds as ERIA which are actually late Antonine or later; but by focussing on the clearly datable material it limits the blurring caused by poorly datable items. For some material types a Flavian versus Antonine division could be sustained, as Macinnes (1989) has attempted, and this exercise would undoubtedly be worth repeating, but it requires more detailed specialist scrutiny of the material than is currently available to make it worthwhile. Here the proposed division allows us to look at the effects of Rome before, during and after the main phases of occupation.

Date	Period
AD 1-75	Late pre-Roman Iron Age (LPRIA)
AD 75-160	Early Roman Iron Age (ERIA)
AD 160-250	Mid Roman Iron Age (MRIA)
AD 250-400	Late Roman Iron Age (LRIA)

Table 1. A chronological scheme for the Scottish Roman Iron Age.

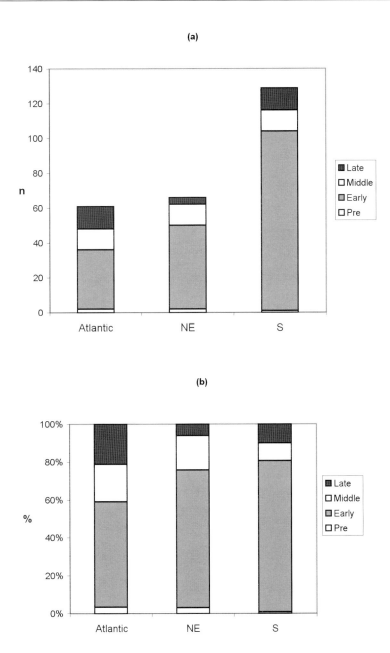

Fig 7 *Comparison of different regions using the chronology set out in table 1. (a) Number of sites with Roman finds of that date; (b) the same information compared as percentages.*

21

Romanisation before the conquest?

There is very little evidence for contact with the Roman world before the Flavian invasion. Only three certain examples are known to the writer: a Langton Down brooch from a burial at Merlsford, Fife, an Aucissa brooch from Dores, Inverness-shire, and a Haltern 70 wine amphora from Gurness, Orkney, all dating to the first half of the first century AD (Hunter 1996, 120-121; Robertson 1970, fig 10.1; Fitzpatrick 1989).[8] With such a small quantity of finds it is unwise to draw wide-ranging conclusions, but it is potentially significant that all lie north of the Forth, perhaps suggesting a deliberate if limited policy of northern contact, or, as Fitzpatrick (1989) has argued, diplomatic relationships with southern tribes who had Roman contacts.

This evidence is very limited compared to that from southern Britain. In southern England there was extensive 'Romanisation before the conquest', with sites such as Silchester and Colchester showing a wealth of pre-Conquest finds, while a series of burials were richly endowed with imported Roman goods (Haselgrove 1984; Stead 1967). Northern England shows less evidence, but still markedly more than Scotland. The picture is dominated by the lowland enclosure complex at Stanwick, North Yorkshire, where the rich and exotic Roman finds point to a major centre of power (Wheeler 1954; Fitts 1998; Fitts et al 1999). No Scottish site (not even Traprain, which is otherwise so dominant) shows such evidence. It may be that the pace of conquest was such that the 'wave of advance' of Roman goods ahead of military conquest had little time to reach Scotland, or that any immediately pre-conquest contact is chronologically indistinguishable from Flavian conquest-period material. In any event, while the north of Britain was clearly not unknown to the classical world, there is at present no sign of significant diplomatic or trading links before the Agricolan invasion.

The vast majority of material falls into the Flavian – Antonine periods (the early Roman Iron Age; ERIA). Fig 7 quantifies sites by the dates of the finds, showing how dominant this period is. By contrast the middle and late Roman periods are markedly sparser; only around 35 finds (site and stray combined) from both the MRIA and the LRIA. It should be admitted that there are potential methodological problems: while the glass has been fully studied (Ingemark 2003), there has been no overall work on the pottery, and further late Roman sherds may lurk in the understudied coarse ware assemblages.[9] However, the marked drop in quantity in the late Roman period appears to be real, as it occurs in detailed studies of both glass and brooches.[10]

Silver for the barbarians – the world of frontier politics, AD 160-250

This more detailed chronological breakdown highlights the late second – early third century (middle Roman Iron Age, MRIA) as a key phase. To understand this, some historical background is necessary. Sometime in the 160s, probably shortly after Antoninus Pius' death in 161, the Antonine Wall was abandoned and the northern frontier was pulled back to Hadrian's Wall (Breeze 1982, 118-124; Hanson & Maxwell 1983, 148-151). There are good grounds for thinking this was linked at least in part to increasing troubles north of the frontier, and for the rest of the second century and the early third there are intermittent literary references to serious problems in the area. Under Commodus in the 180s this became a major worry:

> The greatest war, however, was in Britain. For the tribes in the island crossed the wall which separated them from the Roman army and did a great amount of damage, even cutting down a general together with his troops.
> (Epitome of Dio Cassius LXXII, 8; Ireland 1986, 97-98)

This passage has caused extensive debate, not least in identifying the wall concerned; but a military response was inevitable, allowing Commodus to celebrate a victory. This did not end matters: unrest continued into the reign of Severus. In 197 the governor 'was forced to buy peace from the Maeatae for a large sum' (Epitome of Dio Cassius LXXV, 5, 4; trans Ireland 1986, 109). Ultimately the problems were sufficient to draw the emperor himself to the island, on a journey the Fates had marked as his last one:

> ... the governor of Britain sent word to him that the barbarians were in revolt and that they were over-running the country, looting it and causing widespread havoc
> (Herodian III, 14, 1; Ireland 1986, 110)

Severus came to Britain with a massive army in 208-211. Two campaigns were fought in the north, their focus being the troublesome tribes of the Caledonians and the Maeatae north of the Forth. The armies headed into the north-east, at least as far as the Benvie Water, just south of the Mounth, and may have continued up to the Moray Firth; details are unclear (Breeze 1982, 131-136; Maxwell 1998, 24-26; Birley 1988, 181). However, the campaigns were less than a resounding success, with no major battles fought as the locals engaged in guerrilla tactics; treaties were concluded and almost immediately broken. Severus died in York in 211 and his son and successor, Caracalla 'made peace with the enemy, withdrew from their territory, and abandoned the forts'

(Epitome of Dio Cassius LXXVII, 1, 1; Ireland 1986, 116-117). Whatever arrangements were made, they appear to have been successful; the rest of the third century is a peaceful hiatus in the literary sources until the troublesome Picts rear their heads at the end of it.

While the military campaigns are reflected in the series of marching camps created by the invading armies, the political intrigue before and after is also seen in the archaeology. A series of silver coin hoards, primarily but not exclusively north of the Forth in eastern Scotland, provides archaeological witness to the 'buying of peace' (fig 8). Although often linked purely to the Severan campaigns, their dates suggest this was a long-lived policy running from the 160s to the 230s. Here we can see Roman frontier policy in action, with targeted payments to troublesome areas – although whether this was pay-offs to hostile groups or sweeteners to friendly ones is unclear. It was not a policy restricted to Scotland, but can be found across the northern frontiers of the Empire at this time (Hunter forthcoming a; Todd 1985; Lind 1981; Berger 1996). The hoards range in scale from a handful of coins to almost two thousand. One problematic question is what they were used for. This has been considered in more detail elsewhere (Hunter forthcoming a), but a couple of obvious suggestions can be dismissed: they were not used for trade (there is no evidence of a circulating monetary economy north of the frontier) nor for bullion (since analysis of crucibles shows no sign of silver use until the fourth century; Heald 2005). Instead they are likely to have functioned as status symbols within local society, and perhaps as special-purpose coinage which could be used for restricted transactions such as sealing alliances or marriages, hiring mercenaries or even giving gifts to the gods, much like early Celtic precious metal coinage in southern England (Nash 1978, 7; Haselgrove 1979, 202).

This horizon of silver provides a plausible context for the surprising evidence of the manufacture of forged denarii in Scotland (Holmes & Hunter 2001). Three coin moulds are known from southern and central Scotland, dating to the period c.238-275. They may of course have been intended for fraudulent transactions directed southwards, but a number of features are unusual compared to normal forger's work, and they may equally represent the manufacture of local derivatives for local use (a phenomenon seen also in free Germany; Horsnæs 2003, 337-338). It may be significant that their dates put them in the period after the main denarius hoards, at a time when silver coins were becoming scarce and local versions would meet a need (although the moulds lie largely to the south of the zone of denarius hoarding). This shortage of silver had profound implications which are considered below.

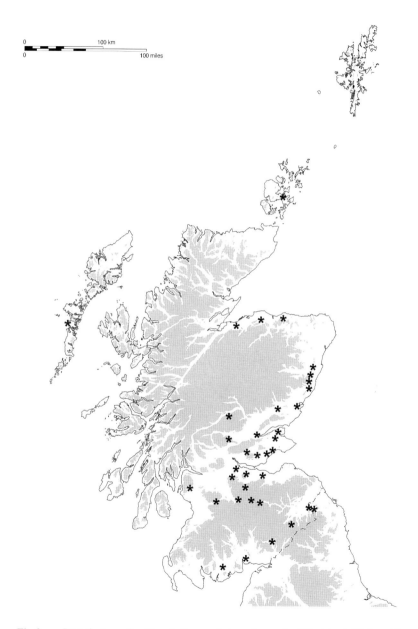

Fig 8   *Distribution of gold and silver coin hoards north of Hadrian's Wall to AD
250, excluding those connected with Roman sites. For details see Hunter
(forthcoming a).*

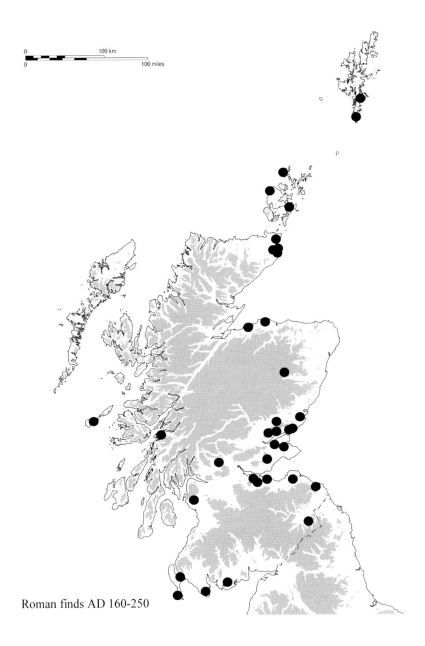

Roman finds AD 160-250

Fig 9 *Distribution of other finds of MRIA date (see Appendix 1).*

It is clear that these frontier politics did not simply involve silver (fig 9; Appendix 1). Hartley (1972, Appendix VIII) noted the disproportionate quantity of late Antonine and later samian from Scottish native sites, especially north of the Forth. Recent study of the glass by Dominic Ingemark has confirmed this trend. Much is of strikingly high quality, notably the exceedingly rare painted drinking cups known from five sites; the four or five vessels of 'snake-thread' glass are another uncommon type (Ingemark 2003, 50-57; forthcoming). By contrast, coarse ware is concentrated south of the Forth, and the material to the south is generally more prosaic, with the inevitable exception of the Traprain Law assemblage.

The preponderance of better-quality material (especially samian and glass) north of the Forth is striking: the distribution is broader than that of the hoards, but it must surely be seen as a deliberate policy in tandem with the coins in an attempt to keep the peace. A similar targeted policy has been argued in detail for north-west Germany by Michael Erdrich (2000), who suggests a changing pattern of contacts with different tribes through time as the politics changed. It is hard to argue this for the earlier Roman period in Scotland, where finds are abundant across the country – or if it was happening, subsequent redistribution within local societies has erased the picture. However, in the late second-early third century we can glimpse a deliberate Roman policy of targeting particular areas.

Bribery at Birnie
This troubled time has been thrown into sharp relief by ongoing excavations at Birnie, Moray (fig 10). Here metal-detecting located 18 *denarii*, probably from a scattered hoard, in a field known from aerial photographs to contain a later prehistoric settlement (Jones et al 1993, pl VIII). This provided a tremendous chance to investigate the setting of such a hoard, to check whether it was indeed contemporary with the cropmarks and, if so, to get a picture of the kind of people who were receiving these 'gifts' from Rome. The bulk of such hoards are old finds where we know little of their setting, and the chance to explore one with modern field techniques is all too rare.

Excavations directed by the writer are still ongoing, but the broad outline is reasonably clear. The site lies on a well-drained and sheltered gravel terrace above the River Lossie, and was home to a long-lived later prehistoric settlement, attested by a cluster of timber roundhouses in a variety of forms (fig 11). Radiocarbon dates are awaited, but it seems to have been a farm which moved around the terrace over the generations and centuries. The artefacts indicate a flourishing Roman Iron Age phase which was the setting for moments of high drama uncovered by the trowel.

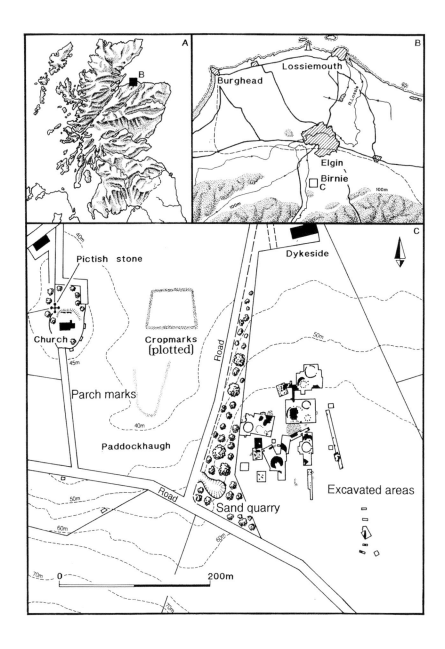

Fig 10 *Location of the site at Birnie, Moray. Drawn by Alan Braby.*

Fig 11 *View of the Birnie excavations, showing one of the well-preserved roundhouses in the background and a medieval building in the foreground. © Author.*

(a)

(b)

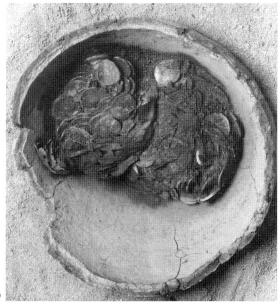

(c)

Fig 12 *The Birnie hoards. (a) Finding the first hoard. (b) The first hoard during laboratory excavation. (c) The second hoard, with the coins in two leather pouches.*

Working with the local detectorist Hamish Stuart, we recorded the locations of stray coins to pinpoint any surviving hoard. A trench was opened around a hotspot in 2000, with more and more scattered coins appearing until, at the base of the ploughsoil, a plough-damaged hoard of some 317 *denarii* was revealed, buried in a locally-made pot (fig 12a-b). This was exciting enough, but the following season our good luck continued: barely ten metres away lay another pot containing an intact hoard of 310 *denarii* in two leather pouches (fig 12c). Some of the coins in the first hoard were also in a pouch, but it was less well preserved. It thus seems that we have potentially four batches of coins buried in two different pots. The latest coin in the first hoard dates to AD 197, while the second discovery ends in 193, and the overall composition supports the idea that the hoards arrived on the site a few years apart (Holmes 2006). This looks like a series of offerings over a number of years. Such stark and regular patterning suggests the hand of Rome lay directly behind this, with little secondary movement between Iron Age groups to blur the patterns. We may speculate on direct connections by sea, with Roman emissaries sailing up to the Moray Firth to deal with local power-brokers.

These transactions were not conducted solely in coin: other finds from the site show a wider spectrum of contacts, with brooches, glass and pottery (fig 6, 25-27). There are four brooches, attractive and unusual examples which reinforce the point that this material was desirable and sought-after, not 'beads for the natives'. An unprepossessing sherd of glass comes from a pillar-moulded bowl – high-quality Roman glass of mid-late first century date (Price & Cottam 1998, 44-46) – while the 2005 excavations uncovered a sherd of Roman kitchenware from a second-century BB1 cooking jar from Dorset. Such everyday pottery was a surprisingly rare import to Iron Age Scotland, whose inhabitants preferred tablewares, and it generally occurs on higher-status sites with a wider range of Roman material. But the star Roman find is a miniature work of art: a small enamelled bird perched on a ring, perhaps a pin-head or a decorative mount (fig 13).

Fig 13 *The Birnie bird mount (length 21 mm).*

This broadens our picture of the site's contacts with the Roman world, stretching back to the first century: these people had built a relationship with Rome which ran for over a hundred years. They also had other connections to the wider world: jewellery of cannel coal points to contacts across the Moray Firth, where Brora in Sutherland is the nearest source, while there are pieces of horse harness imported from southern Scotland or northern England. The site was also a craft centre, smelting and smithing iron and casting bronze – another rare activity, marking the inhabitants as people who could control manufacture rather than wait for someone else to service their needs. Yet the farm was undefended – there were no impressive defences to mark it out in the landscape and show its inhabitants' status. This apparent paradox will be considered later.

The later Roman period, AD 250-400

The evidence suggests that in the MRIA, after the withdrawal from Antonine Scotland, the Romans conducted a deliberate policy of targeting the troublesome tribes of north-east Scotland with diplomatic gifts. How, if at all, did this change in the late Roman period? The quantity of known late Roman finds is markedly less than in the first and second centuries, but about equivalent to the MRIA. The thirty sites and five stray finds currently known are split roughly equally either side of the Forth, but the distribution throws up some interesting questions when compared to earlier phases (fig 14; Appendix 2). Since the material has not all been subject to modern reappraisal the dating is liable to revision, but it offers a useful first pass at the problem. A couple of points are immediately visible. While there is a dramatic drop-off in the number of sites in the south, this is much less marked in the Atlantic, especially in Caithness and the Northern Isles (fig 7). North-east Scotland is all but barren; of the four finds, two (Kintore and Peel; C Wallace, pers comm.; *Britannia* 34 (2003), 302) are from former Roman sites and most probably relate to limited late Roman military reuse.[11] Some of the handful of stray coin finds from the area are doubtless genuine losses which would flesh out the picture; these have not been subjected to detailed autopsy, although a solidus of Honorius from the Meikle Loch, Slains, is included as it is unlikely to be a recent loss (Curtis & Hunter in prep). Given the quantity of earlier Roman material from this area, it is difficult to see this lack simply as a bias in our knowledge. Again this suggests a deliberate Roman policy of targeting certain areas, in this case avoiding the troublesome tribes of the north-east (presumably by now the Picts of the historical sources).

It is always tempting, when arguing for patterns in distributions, to try to explain away exceptions. In fact, given that material would be moving between Iron Age societies as well as coming directly from the Roman world, it would not be a

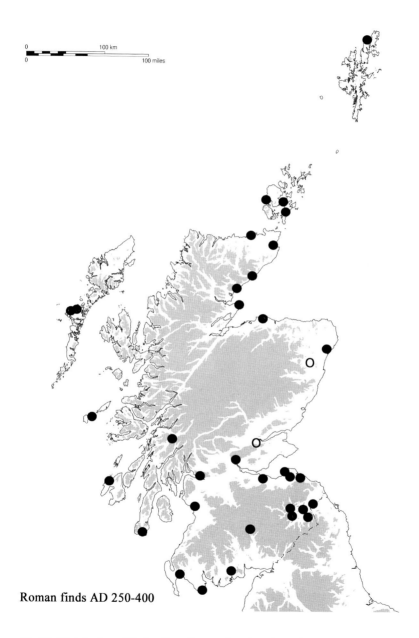

Roman finds AD 250-400

Fig 14 *Distribution of finds of late Roman date (see Appendix 2). Open symbols are probably connected with Roman military activity.*

surprise for some Roman material to end up indirectly in the north-east. However, two further points are perhaps worth noting. The main 'exception' is the Roman material at Sculptor's Cave, Covesea. Here, in these votive deposits, are we seeing the deliberate rejection of Roman material, symbolic now of the enemy? The other point, raised by the Slains solidus, is the occasional occurrence of high-value material – to which the 'Moray Firth' fibula might be added, if we only knew which side of the Firth it came from (see below). Could these represent occasional attempts to tempt individual leaders back into the Roman fold? Or the acquisition of high-value material for votive deposition, echoing the practices at Covesea? But these speculations are little but historical fiction, as the evidence is so sparse. It is as well to accept the apparent shift through time, and accept also that a few exceptions do not invalidate the pattern.

In terms of the material, there is little difference north and south of the Forth (Appendix 2). Pottery predominates, mostly tablewares as in the earlier period, with glass drinking vessels and brooches the other main find categories. None are abundant, but there are hints of a continuing concern with feasting and appearance. Coins feature on a number of sites, although most are single poorly-recorded old finds. However, there are a small number of coin 'hot-spots' in southern Scotland, with hundreds of low-denomination copper alloy coins from each (fig 15): Traprain Law (East Lothian), Springwood (Roxburghshire), Piltanton Burn (Wigtownshire) and Dreghorn (Ayrshire) (Sekulla 1982; Bateson & Holmes 1997, 534; Bateson & Holmes 2003, 248; Robertson 2000, 354, no 1454). All show an extended contact period from the 270s to the end of the fourth century. Apart from the hillfort of Traprain, the nature of these sites is uncertain in the absence of archaeological investigation. However, it would be very surprising if a hillfort did not lie under the medieval castle at Roxburgh, immediately across the Teviot from the Springwood cluster, while the other two findspots are both coastal and could easily serve as trading or contact sites. Given how few late Roman coins turn up on other sites, it is likely that these clusters represent focal places where contact with Rome took place, with small change being used for this; since this had no value in local transactions it did not move off-site in any significant quantities. Other similar sites doubtless remain to be detected; a small collection of late Roman coins recently reported from Sprouston on the Tweed, which emerged as a major centre in the Anglo-Saxon period, suggests this may be another similar site (J W Elliot, pers comm; Bateson & Holmes forthcoming; for the site, see Smith 1991).

Late Roman coin hoards show a similar strong concentration in southern Scotland, with the exception of the lost hoard from Fort Augustus and the votive hoard from Covesea Cave (fig 15; Robertson 2000, no 982, 1359). The quantities involved vary from a few tens to a few hundreds of coins – there is nothing yet on the scale of the

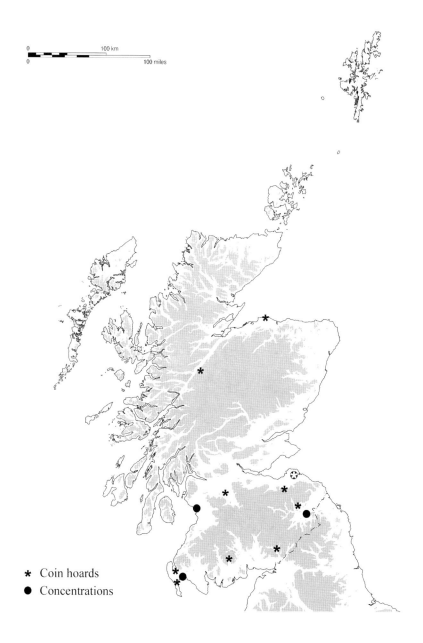

Fig 15 *Distribution of late Roman coin hoards and concentrations of coin finds.*

* Coin hoards
● Concentrations

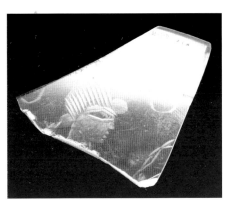

Fig 16 Late Roman engraved glass bowl fragment, Traprain Law. © National Museums of Scotland.

massive southern British late Roman hoards. These hoards have never been properly integrated into the study of the period, but if there were centres of Roman contact in southern Scotland, as argued above, these hoards could represent local wealth, either saved for such transactions or buried as votive offerings because of their powerful connections. It suggests again a difference between south and north of the Forth, with the south participating more directly in contacts with Rome.

While the coins may be low-denomination small change, once again the quality of some of the other objects is striking. There is some very high-quality glass from Traprain (such as an engraved glass bowl with human figures (fig 16), and several claw beakers; Curle & Cree 1916, fig 27; Cree 1923, fig 21), while the gold crossbow brooches from Erickstanebrae, Dumfriesshire and 'the Moray Firth' are some of the finest known from Britain (Curle 1932, 370-371; RIB II.3, 2421.43; Hartley et al 2006, 168). The magnificent bronze vessel hoard from Helmsdale also stands out (Spearman 1990).[12] The southern sites differ in access to material: on the limited sample currently available they tend to have a greater range, most marked at Traprain with its unparalleled rich and extensive late Roman assemblage. In terms of site type, the southern material concentrates strongly on enclosed sites, primarily hillforts, in contrast to the much wider spread of earlier material. The northern material does not predominate on a particular site type, although brochs feature prominently. All bar one of the southern sites show continuity from early to late Roman; this is only true for about half the northern sites.

	S Scotland	NE Scotland	Atlantic Scotland
Early *(AD 75-160)*	Widespread access controlled through existing social hierarchies	Widespread access with some differences between sites	Less extensive access with little consistent control
Middle *(AD 160-250)*	Limited access to quality material except on Traprain	Concentration of quality material	Concentration of quality material
Late *(AD 250-400)*	Continuity and contraction – focus on a few central sites, with little distribution	Almost no material	Continuing access to good-quality material, but not in quantity

Table 2. Patterns of contact with the Roman world through time.

36

Retrospect and prospect

Table 2 attempts to summarise the chronological patterns by area. It must be emphasised that the patterns teased out above are based on a highly insubstantial data set, and future discoveries may well turn them on their head. However, this is what we have, and it is better to use it with reservations than wait perennially for others to deal with it.

Having reviewed the evidence of Roman finds in Iron Age Scotland and tried to look at broad patterns of change through time, what does it mean? The Roman finds cannot be dismissed as trinkets. There is a clear pattern of differential access in the ERIA which indicates these were desirable items whose availability was socially controlled. The strong selectivity of quality items and particular functional types indicates they were valued for particular social purposes, consistent with and developing from existing patterns of display behaviour. The data for AD 160-250 are sparser, but it is clear again that, especially in the north, selected quality material was involved. For the later Roman period there are suggestions of a similar pattern, with an emphasis on tablewares and ornaments. Thus we can suggest that there was a continuing desire for Roman items in local society, and a selection of those items of local use. Whatever the long term impact of this, at the time these were valued and useful objects. This is seen also in the shifting patterns of contact, reflecting a deliberate targeting of particular groups by the Romans – a policy which would only work if Roman material was sought-after. But what was the overall impact of Rome? Here we will consider two specific practical impacts before turning to the key question of lasting social effects.

Recycling Rome – Roman goods as raw materials

While these Roman objects may have been cherished and valued items, everything must pass. Times change, brooch pins break, pots get dropped … and it is clear that many Roman objects had a very practical afterlife. Once broken, they were widely recycled. Many samian sherds show evidence of abrasion (Robertson 1970, 208); they may have been reused as polishers, perhaps for preparing hides, or as sources of pigments.[13] Other sites show evidence of the transformation of Roman vessels into more locally useful forms: the samian bowl from Castlehill, Ayrshire, had its domed base cut out, presumably to form a small cup, while the pottery from Fairy Knowe showed evidence of similar reuse (unpublished observations by writer; Willis 1998a, 330-331). It is often argued (although not yet securely demonstrated) that much of the raw material for making beads and bangles came from Roman glass (e.g. Stevenson 1956a, 215-218; Henderson & Kemp 1992), while recent scientific work has highlighted how widely Roman copper alloys were reused. Dungworth's analysis of north British metalwork showed the widespread recycling of Roman alloys in native-style metalwork, while Andrew Heald's study of non-ferrous metalworking debris such as moulds and crucibles revealed that Roman Iron Age metalworking was dominated by Roman-derived alloys (Dungworth 1996; Heald 2005). Broken brooches went straight into the melting pot, a valuable source of raw material.

The same is true of Roman silver. Heald's work showed no evidence of silver until the late Roman period, but it saw extensive use in the Early Historic period. Since there is no evidence of local production at the time, this silver must be recycled: the source was Roman silver, melted down for reuse from the hoards of hacked-up bullion which came into the country in the late fourth and early fifth century. The magnificent hoard from Traprain is the best example (Curle 1923), but it is unusual mainly because it survives; most would have been melted down. The surviving Roman fragments from the Norrie's Law hoard of Pictish silver point to the fate of most such gifts, providing the raw material for the wealth of silver known in the Early Historic period (Stevenson 1956b).

There was also reuse of more practical Roman commodities, with building stones utilised in souterrains (probably of first-second century date) and in late Roman Iron Age and Early Historic hillfort defences (Hingley 1992, 29; Coleman & Hunter 2002, 92-93; Foster 1998, 14). In both cases there was probably more to this than pragmatism: it has been argued that the reuse was largely symbolic, a desire to identify with icons of Rome's power. There will undoubtedly be further examples, but this should be enough to indicate that one of the legacies of Rome's presence was to provide a wealth of raw material for generations to come.

Roman influence on the origins of Pictish sculpture?

A recurring topic of fascination in Pictish studies has been the origins of Pictish art – or, more specifically, Pictish sculpture. Some years ago the Laings argued that many of the motifs derived ultimately from the Classical world (Laing & Laing 1984). I am deeply sceptical of the artistic sources they identify; but they may be right for the wrong reasons. Was Rome the stimulus for Pictish sculpture, but in terms of the idea rather than the motifs?

This argument is avowedly speculative, but arises from a broader view of stone sculpture in Iron Age Europe. Non-abstract stone carving is largely a phenomenon of and response to contact with the Mediterranean – the statues of Hallstatt and early La Tène Germany, late Iron Age Provence and Iberia (Frey

2000), all areas and periods with strong contacts to the Mediterranean world. This can be seen also in other areas of Gaul, where a tradition of pre-Roman stone and wood sculpture is becoming recognised (Ménez 1999; Deyts 2002; Goudineau 1998; Olivier 2003; Petit & Wahlen 2005; Gomez de Soto & Milcent 2002; Webster 2003, 42-46). Unusually, several come from datable contexts, and this tradition can be shown to date to the second and first centuries BC – the time when Roman influence was becoming felt across Gaul. It is thus likely that both the idea of naturalistic carving and the specific concept of stone sculpture arose from contact with the Roman world.

In Scotland, there is no convincing evidence of a pre-Roman tradition of naturalistic stone-carving. Celtic 'stone heads' are a category beloved by writers on 'Celtic religion', but a critical appraisal shows how slender the dating evidence is. None of the Scottish examples (e.g. Ross 1974; Dodds 1978; Cowie 1986) comes from a secure pre-Roman context. Of course this charge can also be levelled at much of our finest Celtic metalwork, but the problem here is that the significance and depiction of the human head is cross-cultural, not Celtic; and medieval and later folk art abounds with examples of 'Celtic heads' which are stylistically hard to differentiate from supposedly earlier examples (Billingsley 1998, esp. 14-16). More generally, Catherine Johns (2003) has criticised the ready acceptance of 'Celtic traditions' behind more naïve depictions, much of which is better seen in technical terms as the product of craft-workers who were not trained in a Classical, naturalistic tradition. This is not to make value-judgements over these pieces, or to simplify the motives behind them – but the technical challenge of naturalistic carving is not to be under-estimated, by contrast with the ease with which 'Celtic heads' may be produced.

Where does this leave the argument of Roman influence? It is too simplistic to make a bipolar distinction between the abstraction of Celtic art and the naturalism of the Classical world. Much Iron Age art contains naturalistic references transformed into patterns, rather than being truly abstract (Fitzpatrick forthcoming): behind the swirls and spirals, we can recognise animals and sometimes even humans, reflections of the 'Cheshire Cat' nature of this art, where little is left of the beast but its smile (Megaw 1970, 273-274). This may be seen in the human mask on the horns from Torrs, Kirkcudbrightshire, and the bird heads on the accompanying cap (Atkinson & Piggott 1955, 222-223, fig 4, pl LXXIV); it is also seen in the stylised horse-heads which can be read into the designs of many north British bridle bits (e.g. MacGregor 1976, nos 2, 5, 7, 10; the design within one ring represents the eyes, and the bar of the side-link its muzzle). Yet this is markedly different from the direct naturalism of both Roman art and (at some remove) later Pictish art. While the linear derivation of Pictish motifs from Roman art, as the Laings proposed, seems flawed, the real Roman influence may lie in the very idea of naturalistic art (as suggested also for Scandinavia; Petersen 2003, 286-287). Indeed we may start to glimpse the beginnings of this habit in the Roman Iron Age.

This strand of the emerging thread takes us to animal art in Scotland outwith the Pictish heartlands. There is a series of poorly-dated animal representations from around Scotland. Broch-period pottery (broadly c. 200 BC – AD 200) includes a few sherds bearing figures of deer (MacGregor 1976, nos 327, 329-331); there are sparse representations from portable material culture, such as the wooden deer head ?handle from Dun Bharabhat, Lewis, also of this date (Harding & Dixon 2000, fig 34.1). Much more speculatively, we may consider here a number of undated rock-carvings, primarily of deer, which Thomas (1961, 20-24, fig 5-6) collated and argued to be a widespread north British tradition with its origins in the Roman Iron Age (fig 17).[14]

A Roman Iron Age dating is supported by a further example from the early excavations on Traprain Law, East Lothian (fig 18). On a block of cannel coal, gathered for jewellery manufacture and partly shaped before being discarded, is a graffito. The later working has destroyed part of it, but confident incised lines define the erect neck, legs and sloping back of an animal facing left, with some definition of anatomical detail on the body; its form suggests a deer. Dating of

Fig 17 Animal carvings, Eggerness, Wigtownshire. © Author.

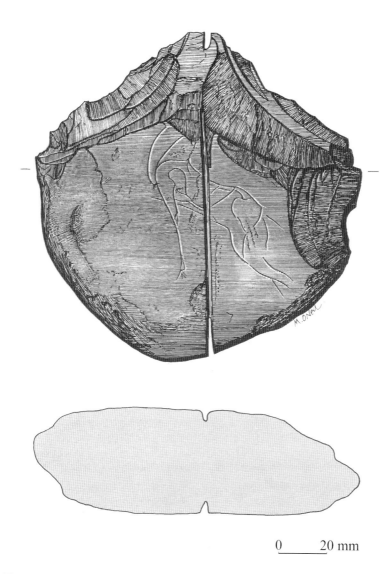

0 _____ 20 mm

Fig 18 *Block of cannel coal from Traprain Law with the incised graffito figure of a deer. The deer was lightly inscribed in outline, with internal detailing, on a natural block. A start was then made to sawing the block in half, but this was abandoned in favour of flaking to round and thin it in order to produce a blank, perhaps for a bangle. However it was abandoned in the process. NMS GV 1562; 138 x 135 x 43 mm. Found in 1914 in section A1, second level (Curle 1915; not published). Drawn by Marion O'Neil.*

41

finds from Traprain is tricky, but this block is from levels which produced Roman material; Curle (1915, 145) mentions samian, suggesting a second century AD *terminus post quem*.

While the whole argument currently remains on circumstantial foundations, there is a growing case to answer for naturalistic art in Scotland arising around the time of contact with Rome. The parallels adduced earlier for naturalism in the Iron Age art of Germany, Mediterranean France and Iberia point to contacts with the Mediterranean world as a causal factor. Hicks (1993) has similarly argued for the origins of Pictish animal art arising from knowledge of the art of Roman Britain, boosted by Christian iconography. This process parallels the development of the first scripts in northern and western Europe, ogam and runes, in response to contact with Latin literacy (Thomas 1994, 30-34; Stoklund 2003, 172-173). A suggestion for further argument is thus that the emergence of Pictish art, in naturalistic concept rather than detail, is due to contact with Rome.

Social changes

The key question posed at the start of this work was the testing of Mann's (1974) hypothesis that the emergence of the Picts arose from a coalition of smaller-scale units in the face of the threat of Rome. Can we identify change in this crucial third-fourth century period, and if so, what was the role of Rome? We have considered the Roman finds, looking at their use in local societies, identifying changes through time and seen the hand of Roman diplomacy behind this, with a policy of targeting or excluding particular areas. What effect did this have? To consider any longer-term impact we must look at developments before and after (as far as the inadequate chronology of Iron Age Scotland allows us), between c. 100 BC and AD 400. The crucial area is north-east Scotland, but we should first look to other areas of Scotland as comparanda.

There is no single narrative of change: instead there are a series of regional and local narratives, some better understood than others. At one level we can make a broad highland-lowland division. In the Atlantic zone, there were significant changes during this period. On most commentators' views, although the origins of brochs lie substantially earlier, the pinnacle of constructing the most complex broch towers should lie within this period, perhaps focussed in the last two centuries BC (Armit 2003, 51-54, 107-108). In Orkney and Caithness this is also the time of the broch villages, clusters of smaller structures around the brochs which surely imply local social hierarchies. By AD 100, it seems broch construction had ceased, although occupation continued within these structures for centuries to come. A series of smaller-scale architectural forms had by this time developed, including wheelhouses (whose chronology remains debated) and later, more irregular cellular structures.

These architectural changes are highly significant in social terms, not least the implication that, with the demise of the brochs, extravagant architecture was no longer seen as the way to show status and identity (Armit 1997b, 252-253; Sharples 2003). It seems there was a shift to a more personal scale of status expression, with architecture focussed inwardly on the users and their visitors rather than outwardly on the viewers. By the fifth or sixth century, Armit has argued that the evidence does indeed point to larger-scale political units, with much of the Western Isles and Shetland in thrall to chiefs based on Orkney (Armit 1990c, 207-208). Yet in this time of change there was also considerable continuity. This is seen especially in the persistence of settlement location on many sites, as witnessed in the extensive post-broch activity common in the area, and testified dramatically at sites like Jarlshof and Scatness on Shetland or Beirgh on Lewis. As far as archaeology can tell, settlement continued without a recognisable gap.

This visible continuity stands in marked contrast to the lowland zone. Many earlier site-types apparently fell from use in the third and fourth centuries. This was stated most dramatically in Peter Hill's study of the unenclosed stone-built 'Votadinian-style' roundhouses so typical of the late pre-Roman and early Roman Iron Age in south-east Scotland. He noted the absence of late Roman finds from most of these sites, and argued for a phase of extensive abandonment (Hill 1982a, 8-12). Other evidence shows similar trends. The exotic architecture of the lowland Scottish brochs does not appear to survive far into the third century, if at all (Macinnes 1984), and the same is true of the souterrains of Angus, Perthshire and Fife (Armit 1999). These phenomena are not as tightly dated as some would wish: the Roman finds from souterrains suggest a range of abandonment dates from the late first to the early third century AD (Coleman & Hunter 2002, 97), while the absence of later Roman finds on these and the Votadinian sites may be due to more limited supply (and thus tighter control of access) – although Hill argued against this from the stratigraphy of the finds, where known, and LRIA radiocarbon dates are lacking from excavated souterrain sites (see below). However, there is no doubt that in lowland Scotland there are severe difficulties in finding the settlements of the third to fifth centuries AD.

This is supported by a provisional analysis of radiocarbon dates in this period, courtesy of Patrick Ashmore. Figure 19 shows the cumulative probabilities of all 'reasonable' radiocarbon dates[15] and then a broad regional division into northern, eastern and western.[16] It is striking that, while the northern area shows a broad plateau through the Roman Iron Age, both eastern and western areas

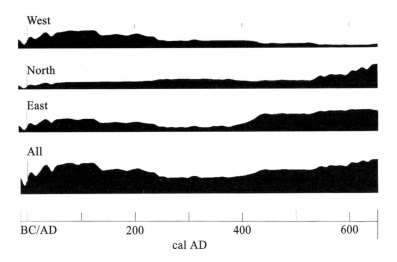

Fig 19 *Plot of the cumulative probabilities of radiocarbon dates in different areas of Scotland; for details see text. Courtesy of Patrick Ashmore.*

show a pronounced dip from a high around AD 1-200 (the rise in eastern Scottish dates after AD 400 largely stems from long cist cemeteries). There do thus appear to be significant changes in the lowlands in the LRIA. While some sites show later activity (e.g. the poorly-dated post-souterrain buildings at Carlungie I and Ardestie; Wainwright 1963; Harding 2004, 240-242) most do not, with recent excavations suggesting these were the exception rather than the rule; the presence of individual later radiocarbon dates on some sites is not a convincing indicator of continuity in the absence of accompanying structures (*contra* Watkins 1984, 68-69).

The patterns are still poorly focussed, and their interpretation cannot be certain: for instance, they may reflect a drop in population, shift in settlement or concentration onto fewer sites. As noted above, the late Roman finds in the south concentrate on hillforts. Some southern hillforts clearly stayed in use throughout the Roman Iron Age, and a few emerge as Early Historic power centres, notably Dumbarton Rock and Edinburgh Castle. In contrast, the north-east shows very little LRIA activity, at the very time when the historical sources speak of restless natives. So where were the Picts?

The Iron Age of the north-east

The 'Pictish homelands' of north-east Scotland have been badly under-studied, with little excavation compared to other parts of the country. It is thus possible that the sparsity of LRIA material is due to limited excavation; certainly the late Roman material in votive deposits at the Sculptor's Cave, Covesea, Moray shows the area was not totally barren (Benton 1931; Shepherd 1993, 80-81). But in recent years there have been quite a number of Iron Age excavations in the area, some very substantial; while many await full analysis and publication, the later Roman Iron Age remains vestigial and elusive. When taken with the marked disparity between early-mid Roman and late Roman finds, there seems to be a case to answer. Mann (1974) suggested that the effect of Rome was to coalesce smaller political units into larger ones. We might expect this to be reflected in the emergence of regional-scale distributions of material culture and the development of larger-scale power centres. Can these be observed?

Artefacts
Turning first to the material culture, there is a clearly-marked regional identity – but this was already in place by the first and second centuries AD. It is seen in particular in the 'massive metalwork' tradition from the Forth to the Moray Firth, a flourishing style of Celtic metalwork characterised especially by big, bold personal ornaments (fig 20; MacGregor 1976, 104, 184-185; Ralston

Fig 20 *Selection of massive metalwork.* © *National Museums of Scotland.*

1979, 482-483; Hunter forthcoming c). Indeed the emergence of this distinctive style at this time may be connected to the effect of Rome, with the perceived threat leading to a reinforcing of local identity (see Hunter forthcoming b). This evidence points to an existing regional tradition and some shared concept of identity, at least at the elite level of metalwork-consumers, before the Pictish period.

This is not to suggest that the area was a single coherent entity. Throughout prehistory and early history the north-east persistently shows a bipartite division to either side of the Mounth, that great geological barrier (Maxwell 1987, 32; *ibid* 1990, fig 6). For the Iron Age we may note particular styles of glass beads which are a product of the northern region, while massive metalwork shows evidence of northern and southern sub-styles (Guido 1978, 85-89; MacGregor 1976, 107-108; Kilbride-Jones 1980, 154). These styles do not indicate political unity over this huge area, but show an area where groups shared their cultural traditions. However, it illustrates a strong degree of regional identity well before the appearance of the Picts.

These regional traditions of material culture changed in the LRIA. There is no evidence that the beads or the metalwork continued far into the third century; the dating evidence for both points strongly to a first-second century AD floruit. Of course there is the risk of circularity here; given the lack of late Roman finds, dating anything (especially stray finds of metalwork) to this period is difficult. But it is supported by the lack of any association between the massive metalwork tradition and what followed. The material culture of the early Pictish period has long been elusive, but work by Heald (2001), building on that of Laing and Laing (1986), has identified a range of items which can now be seen to start in the third-fourth centuries and continue into the seventh century or so. The key items are massive terrets, knobbed spearbutts, 'jet' bobble-heads for pins or (more likely) gaming pieces, and a range of developed projecting ring-headed pins, culminating in hand-pins. Their differences from massive metalwork are striking. Firstly, the material itself is markedly more prosaic than the artistic achievements of the massive tradition. The distribution is also very different. Rather than a regional tradition, we see the emergence of styles linking north Britain and Ireland, which also occur (rarely) on southern British sites (fig 21).[17] This Irish connection was rare in the earlier period; there are exceptions, but given the geographical closeness the absence of Irish-style metalwork in Scotland and vice versa is more striking than the few examples, especially in comparison to the widespread links attested in earlier prehistory and in the late first millennium AD (*contra* Raftery 2005). Laing and Laing (1986) link these new connections to the *conspiratio barbarica* of 367, when Picts, Scots and the elusive Attacotti descended on the province. Rather than

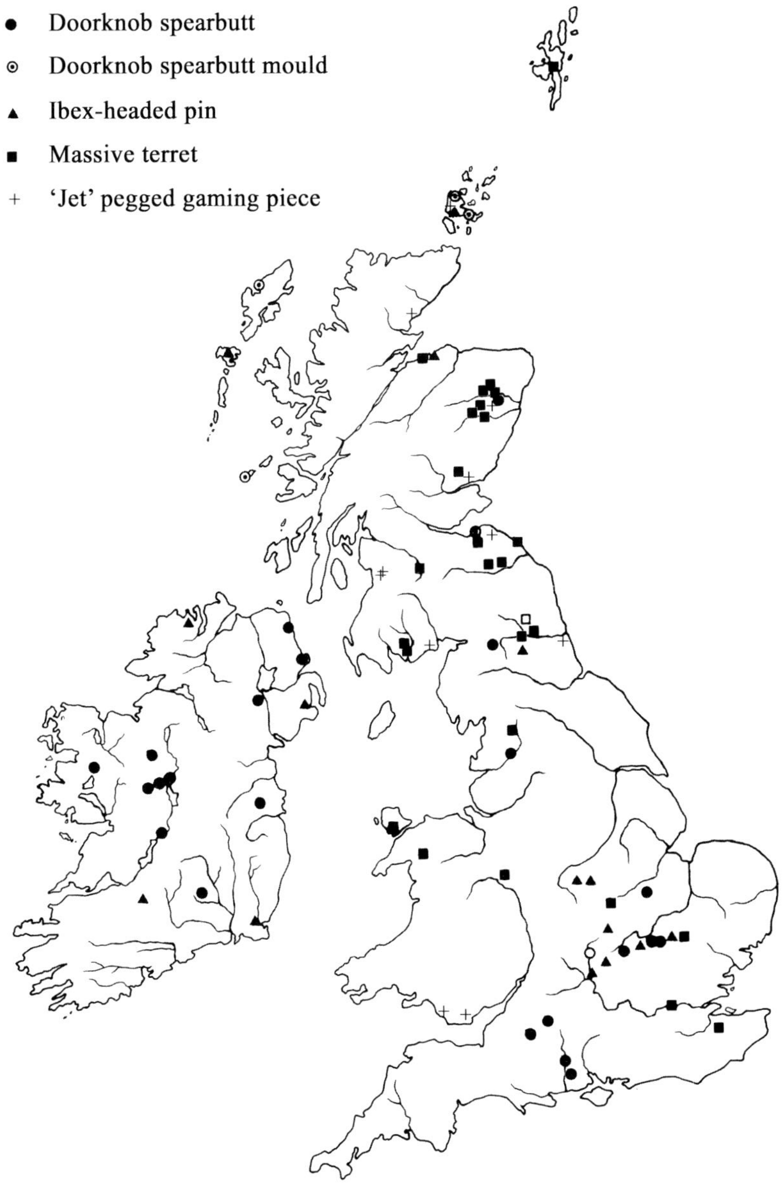

● Doorknob spearbutt

⊙ Doorknob spearbutt mould

▲ Ibex-headed pin

■ Massive terret

+ 'Jet' pegged gaming piece

Fig 21 *Distribution of material culture of third-seventh century AD date (from Heald 2001, fig 3, with additions).*

such direct correlations to history, however, it is better to see this as a wider process of increasing links to Ireland, southern Scotland and beyond. This suggests changing political alliances.

With all this evidence a degree of caution is required. There can be many factors behind artefact distributions, and the regional spreads are unlikely to represent politically-coherent units; they recur repeatedly in north-east prehistory and proto-history, as noted. It could be argued that these contacts provided the natural preconditions for political amalgamation, with the creation of wide-ranging connections at certain social levels, spawned or encouraged by the proximity of Rome. In this view, such visual display items as the massive metalwork, while a natural sociological response to the threat posed by Rome, were of little relevance after this formative period, once larger political units had formed and been accepted. Yet the total lack of a distinctively Pictish material culture in this formative LRIA period argues against this. We see not a Pictish identity but much wider connections being displayed, and the character of the material is less markedly elite than what went before. Does this represent amalgamation, or a major social shift? We can turn to the settlement evidence for another angle.

Settlements
As with the artefacts, regional settlement patterns are apparent well before the Pictish period. For instance, souterrains were common across the area, differentiated from those to north and west by their size (Armit 1999, illus 1; Miket 2002, fig 24).[18] The distribution of oblong timber-framed forts also points to a particular north-east type, although their dating is much debated (Ralston et al 1983, 161-162; Feachem 1966, 67-68; Gentles 1993; Alexander 2002). There are broader patterns as well. In contrast to southern Scotland, there is a marked preponderance of unenclosed over enclosed sites in the north-east (Maxwell 1983, 30-32; Macinnes 1982), although there has been no consensus on interpretation. Some see this as indicating a more locally-based level of organisation, others as signifying the presence of a few large regional centres which exercised a considerable degree of control (Childe 1935, 255-257; Armit 1997a, 61). Crucial to this argument are the hillforts and other enclosed sites (Ralston 2004). Regrettably we lack a framework for understanding them, as there has been very little work on the major enclosed sites of the area. However, the only substantial recent excavation in the area, on the Caterthuns (Angus), found no evidence to suggest these were densely occupied centres. While some of the smaller sites (such as the promontory fort of West Mains of Ethie on the Angus coast; Wilson 1980) show evidence of occupation in the Roman Iron Age, the larger ones can perhaps be seen as places to visit rather than to live – foci which drew surrounding communities together at key times of year. But this

is a picture painted from a limited palette: there is a crying need for further work on the enclosed sites of the area, with such visually dominant sites as Tap o'Noth, Bennachie and Dunnideer all essentially untested by the spade. Without an understanding of these foci, it is hard to interpret the wider picture.

While accepting these limitations, on current evidence settlement in the north-east is best seen as based on small units, with larger sites acting as foci where groups would gather at certain times but which were not necessarily elite power centres. There were probably local hierarchies: south of the Mounth, the finds suggest that the broch sites were of a greater status than the souterrain sites, the latter being the typical farms of the area (Coleman & Hunter 2002, 97-98). Yet important sites need not have an architectural signature – at Birnie, with its lack of defences, it is the finds and not the architecture which mark it as a site of importance.[19] But how significant were these status sites? They may well have been quite limited in their influence. We do not know how many Birnie-type sites lurk within the plethora of similar undifferentiated cropmarks (Jones et al 1993), but the occurrence of other *denarius* hoards in nearby valleys suggests Rome was dealing with a series of local leaders along the Moray Firth. This is supported by the surviving quantities of massive metalwork; if these were elite possessions, there were lots of elite about. Any hierarchies here appear to be quite small-scale.

As the radiocarbon evidence reviewed earlier suggests, this settlement pattern apparently saw an abrupt disruption in the later Roman Iron Age. Most excavated sites show no sign of activity after the early third century AD. This impression is confirmed by the results of recent, more extensive campaigns of investigation. At Kintore (Aberdeenshire), large-scale examination of over 18 ha of landscape has identified a pattern of shifting settlement from the middle Bronze Age to the late pre-Roman Iron Age, with a dramatic gap in the first six centuries AD (M Cook, pers comm.). Here the absence in the E-MRIA apparently reflects the imposition and lasting impact of a Roman temporary camp on the area, but the LRIA gap is repeated in Edinburgh University's series of excavations in Angus. Full synthetic publication is in preparation, but again the results have shown many sites with activity in the first and second centuries AD, but nothing to fill the later third-fifth century gap (A Dunwell, pers comm).[20]

Here it is worth recalling Whittington & Edwards' (1993) pollen work which suggested woodland regeneration at their sample sites in Fife and Aberdeenshire in the first few centuries AD. This would represent a different pattern from the extensive clearances of the late pre-Roman and early Roman Iron Age seen in southern Scotland and northern England (Tipping 1997). Further pollen work to clarify this trend would be very desirable: it is based on three sites in an area which is otherwise a black hole for pollen studies (Tipping 1994, illus 2).

By the Early Historic period proper this settlement gap was filled, at least in part, by a renewed phase of enclosed sites (Alcock 1987, fig 4). Yet the available dates for these sites do not (with the possible exception of Burghead) suggest origins as early as the third-fourth centuries AD. No other enclosed sites excavated so far in the north-east (primarily coastal promontory forts) have produced late Roman Iron Age dates, and Alcock's wider campaign of excavations on Early Historic enclosed sites also showed little or no evidence of LRIA origins. Thus there remains a gap. At the moment it can be filled by only a handful of sites, notably the ritual site at Sculptor's Cave, Covesea; the open cropmark sites seem to tail off, and the enclosed sites do not develop for another two or three centuries. Commercial archaeology is revealing some activity of this period, for instance at Lesmurdie Road, Elgin[21], but this appears to be a virgin site with no continuity from the ERIA.

While further work will undoubtedly improve and modify our picture, there is a disjuncture between the settlement patterns which had developed in the centuries leading up to the third century AD, and the settlements of the Pictish period 'proper'. Other categories of evidence show similar dislocations, at least north of the Mounth (Shepherd 1983, 331-332). Taken with the shifts noted in material culture it suggests a major change, with dislocation of settlements (and presumably thus inheritance systems) and contact networks. Here the evidence from Birnie will be of key importance: we know there was activity on the site in the early third century, and the question of whether it continued in use or was abandoned is a central one to be tested.

The impact of Rome?

Having looked at the artefactual evidence for Roman contact and reviewed other categories of evidence, we can return to our core question. Without the historical sources, would we identify the LRIA as a time of change? The answer is a qualified yes – only in some areas of the country. In the Atlantic, while there was a process of change, this appears to have been evolutionary rather than dramatic. The lowlands show more marked change. In both the south and the north-east, the number of dated sites drops off and Celtic-style metalwork ceased to be produced, while late Roman finds are markedly fewer than early Roman ones. In the south this may be interpreted as a time of contraction and continuity: the later finds occur on central sites such as hillforts which were also used in the earlier period. Roman finds still marked out the important sites in contemporary society, but with the reduced quantities available they were retained by the local elite rather than distributed within wider society; they were now more exclusive. In the north-east, there was more dramatic change. Apart from the disappearance of distinctive regional metalwork, settlements become archaeologically invisible and souterrains were abandoned. All this points to significant changes. But how far can this be attributed to Rome?

We have seen that in the earlier period, Roman goods were selectively adopted to fit into existing social mechanisms. The lifestyles of people may have adapted somewhat to the possibilities of this new material, but in broad terms it was fitted into existing ways of life. Roman finds were undoubtedly important, as a crucial part of contemporary social practice and a power resource in dealing with others; they may have led to (or accentuated) shifts in behaviour, such as focussing power into fewer hands, but these were part of wider trends. The variety in Roman finds between different settlements points to regional social differences in their circulation and use. Thus they were probably more crucial in the more hierarchical south-east than in the Atlantic. However, any lasting impact is a more complex question. In the Atlantic this may have been limited. While Roman finds were valued (as seen in the extensive repair to some, such as the Okstrow samian or the Midhowe bronze vessel), it is hard to see such low quantities having a paramount role in social interaction. Indeed the small quantities suggest irregular supply, which would be an unstable basis for incorporation into local power politics. They undoubtedly had a role, but perhaps more as desiderata than essentials.

In the south, contact with Rome had an importance throughout the Roman Iron Age. In the late Roman period, although less prevalent than in earlier times, this continued to play an important role. This is seen in the concentration of finds on certain sites. Whatever the precise role of hillforts, it seems they were the focal sites of the period in this area. This is clearest for Traprain Law, with its wealth of Roman finds (most notably the great silver hoard) but other sites produce similar late material, such as Edinburgh Castle and Eildon Hill North. In a general dearth of settlement evidence, they stand out.

But what of the north-east, the main area of interest in tracing the emergence of the Picts? What role did Rome have in these dramatic LRIA changes? We can suggest a number of models.

- The lack of late Roman finds arose from conscious rejection of Roman goods. These societies became antagonistic towards Rome, and no longer wanted to play a part in these frontier politics.

- The lack of late Roman finds was a deliberate Roman policy. It was designed to destabilise societies which had grown dependent on Roman finds for displaying their power and status. This could lead to two main outcomes: antagonism towards Rome on the part of existing elites; or the undermining and collapse of these elites and their replacement by a new social order.

• The lack of late Roman finds was accident rather than design. Internal developments within local societies meant the old guard of local elites, who had dealt with Rome, no longer held power – perhaps because of discontent at the wealth they acquired from Rome.

• The Roman finds were irrelevant. Longer-term social processes, in which Roman goods were involved but not dominant, led to the development of more overarching elites. This may have been a response to the threat of Rome. Distinctive material culture was no longer necessary: its role, crucial in the earlier phase of transition, was superseded. Objects now showed new alliances, to similar large-scale groups elsewhere beyond the frontier.

Doubtless other models could be devised, or the elements combined in other ways. But does our evidence allow us to choose between the varied possibilities?

The evidence as it stands suggests major change in several areas: the disappearance of pre-existing indigenous material culture, a marked drop-off and discontinuity in settlement, and a steep decline in the availability of Roman goods. Change in both settlement and material culture argues strongly that this was no minor event. This makes it less likely that the very visual art of the metalwork became redundant because a new 'Pictish' identity no longer required visual display, as the settlement evidence does not support continuity. Such a dramatic change as the one proposed here is best seen as a major social disruption. The kinds of people who could commission massive metalwork, and the farming systems which could generate surpluses to fill souterrains, were no more. What took their place is unclear, but its difference was expressed in the material culture, showing increasingly wide connections outside the region. This may be seen not as amalgamation, but fracture; a basic change in the social and political structures, with changing affiliations becoming clear. It is perhaps no surprise that the sources record increasing Pictish wars in the fourth century: at a time of such social upheaval, warfare (or militarism) would not be unexpected, and the widespread connections of the material culture lend archaeological substance to the 'barbarian conspiracies'. Indeed Armit (1999, 594) has commented that warfare was the 'principal surviving means by which status could be demonstrated and social bonds maintained' – although it is archaeologically invisible if this is so.

But this does not explain why such dramatic change occurred. Was it really caused by Rome? If there was a changing Roman policy, firstly to target the north-east and then to avoid it, would this really be enough to undermine local society? This could be the case if the availability of Roman goods had led to a 'prestige goods economy', where societies became dependent on Roman goods in their expressions of power and status. Is this plausible?

In quantitative terms the amount of mid-Roman material (AD 160-250) is less than that from the earlier period; and compared to the wealth of contemporary Scandinavian burials, the few poorly-equipped north-east burials look rather sad. What was different, however, was silver, in the form of coinage. Little silver came into native hands until the late second century; then suddenly this new prestige good came to play a major role as the Romans plied local elites with it. While other Roman goods could be accommodated in existing lifestyles, this was a new material, leading to new responses. We have already considered its possible roles in local society, and it can best be understood as a prestige good, a special-purpose coinage which oiled the wheels of elite social transactions. The time period involved, some two or three generations, would be enough for silver to become normal, a standard part of local display behaviour; indeed it may have had a value beyond this, as a token of Rome's favour to certain groups. If silver had become an integrated part of local social behaviour, then its deliberate withdrawal could have occasioned considerable problems.

We cannot hope to reconstruct the details of local politics, for instance in pro- and anti-Roman factions, or in the details of Roman dealings with them, perhaps cutting contact to one group and boosting another (as Erdrich (2000) has suggested for other areas). It remains but a theory that the silver was so crucial; it may simply be blinding our modern eyes with its gleam. It is possible that, while Roman material culture and Roman politics were a factor, they were not the determining one. The Roman finds became part of a system which involved considerable display activities (notably with elaborate metalwork), but lacked a marked social hierarchy except at a fairly local level. Perhaps this community of competing equals was simply unsustainable, too big a drain on the available resources or too tempting for others eyeing it up enviously.

This will remain a topic of debate; the arguments made here, while hopefully plausible, are open to debate. Yet there are patterns in the evidence, changes in several areas which broadly correlate; and the persistent, recurring factor is Rome. Our knowledge of the north-east Iron Age, and of its relations with the Roman world, will undoubtedly continue to develop. But I argue here that it is Rome, and specifically Roman political interference, which was crucial in building these societies up and then bringing them down.

Conclusions

It must be admitted that there are no certain answers, and the dataset remains very sparse. Yet there is no harm in trying to use the data we have and set up models for testing, rather than forever gathering information. The persistence of Mann's theory of a Pictish confederacy shows the value of pushing the available data. Yet it has seen no detailed archaeological scrutiny until now; and the results are far from a ringing endorsement. The amalgamation theory is not readily supported by archaeological analysis in our current state of knowledge. The north-east already had an existing regional identity by the ERIA; it was not created with the emergence of the Picts. Indeed this regional identity disappears when Picts emerge into history, to be replaced by artefacts showing wider affiliations. This could be read as evidence of wider polities, although these new objects are markedly unspectacular compared to the earlier metalwork. However, there is no sign of any concentration of power, nor of the emergence of visible elites. If there was a shift from locally-based power (on sites like Birnie) to more direct regional control in the LRIA then the evidence is likely to lie in the enclosed sites. Yet their origins, as far as we yet know, seem to lie later, from the fifth/sixth century onwards.

Rather than an amalgamation, the evidence may instead be read as a crisis: a major social and political crash, caused by Rome creating tensions between 'haves and have-nots'; building these groups up, and then pulling them down. With both models, it is ironic that the unintended consequence was the emergence of powerful groups who became a major threat – a scenario which resonates with colonial adventures in more recent history.

Attempts to confirm, deny or develop these ideas will take years to come and require much more work. Indeed, further clues are likely to lie in the soil at Birnie itself. It is perhaps foolhardy to be floating such schemes before completing excavation. Yet such model-building provides us with ideas to test, and makes it harder to approach an excavation unthinkingly. And whatever the detailed explanation, the patterns suggest one thing quite clearly. In the late third century, the Picts were new players on the block, not the old players with a different name. While the population may not have changed, and we need not invoke the migrations so beloved of early scholars, the Picts represent the emergence of new power structures in the north which are radically different from what went before – and which remain an intellectual challenge.

Acknowledgements
This Groam House Museum lecture was delivered in Rosemarkie on 9th May 2003, and I am grateful to the Directors of the Groam House Museum for the opportunity to develop my thoughts on this fascinating topic, to the audience that evening for their participation, and to Susan Seright for her patience and forbearance in its lengthy transformation into a written format. Aspects of the argument have subsequently been developed and road-tested before the Nineteenth Congress of Roman Frontier Studies in Pécs, Hungary (Hunter 2005), the First Millennia Studies Group, the Pictish Arts Society, the Moray Society, and the Glasgow University Seminar series, in both lecture theatres and bars, and I am grateful to those audiences for comments which have refined the argument. A number of excavators (mentioned individually in the text) have kindly supplied information on their sites in advance of publication, while Jenny Shiels and Stuart Campbell have been of considerable assistance in providing details of recent Treasure Trove finds. Patrick Ashmore readily took up the challenge of assessing whether the radiocarbon evidence supported my ideas, and I am grateful for his initial findings. Examination of Orcadian material was made possible thanks to a grant from the Mona Sinclair fund of the Orkney Heritage Society. Craig Angus assisted with graphical work, scanning and setting many of the illustrations for publication, while Tanja Romankiewicz helped me retain some sense of perspective on matters Pictish. Valuable advice has been received from Nick Holmes on coinage and Colin Wallace on pottery; he has discussed the results of his work on late Roman pottery in advance of publication, and also commented on the text to its marked advantage. David Breeze, David Clarke and Andrew Heald also read and commented on the text, saving me from a number of factual follies, stylistic foibles and interpretative fudges. As ever, responsibility for the final result resides with the writer.

Appendix 1 - mid Roman finds, AD 160-250

Coin hoards are excluded, as these are listed in Hunter forthcoming a.

Site	County	Find(s)	Site type	Reference
Waulkmill	Aberdeen	Glass stemmed beaker/flask	Burial	Curle 1932, 390-391 Holmes & Hunter 2001, 174 Ingemark forthcoming
Airlie	Angus	Glass cup	Burial	Davidson 1886
Carlungie I	Angus	Gauloise 12 amphora	Souterrain	Wainwright 1963, 147 Fitzpatrick 2003, 63
Carlungie II	Angus	Brooch	Souterrain	Wainwright 1953, pl. XVI
Hurly Hawkin	Angus	Samian; sestertius of Geta	Broch & souterrain	Hartley 1972, 55; Robertson 1971, 117
Pitcur I	Angus	Samian	Souterrain	Hartley 1972, 54-55
Redcastle	Angus	Glass cup	Souterrain	Ingemark 2005
Dun Mor Vaul, Tiree	Argyll	Glass painted cup	Broch	MacKie 1974, 148-149
Dunollie	Argyll	Glass painted cup	Hillfort	Alcock & Alcock 1987, 142, ill 9 no 102
Castlehill	Ayr	Samian	Hillfort	Hartley 1972, 54
Kirk Hill, St Abbs	Berwick	Coarse ware	Promontory fort	Hogg 1945 (identification not entirely secure)
Everley	Caithness	Samian	Broch	Hartley 1972, 55
Keiss Harbour	Caithness	Samian	Broch	Hartley 1972, 54
Keiss Road	Caithness	Samian	Broch	Hartley 1972, 55
Nybster	Caithness	Samian	Broch	Hartley 1972, 54
Traprain Law	E Lothian	Samian, glass	Hillfort	Hartley 1972, 55 Ingemark forthcoming
Auchterderran	Fife	Denarius of Pertinax	Enclosure	Macdonald 1918, 238
Clatchard Craig	Fife	Samian	Hillfort	Close-Brooks 1986, 155
Hallow Hill	Fife	Glass cups	Burial	Proudfoot 1996, 420-422
Brighouse Bay	Kirkcudbright	Coin mould	Sand dune/ midden	Boon 1994 Holmes & Hunter 2001
Edinburgh Castle	Midlothian	Coarse ware	Hillfort	Hartley 1997, 134 no 21
Kaimes Hill	Midlothian	Severan denarius	Hillfort	Holmes 2004
Covesea	Moray	Glass – snake-thread	Cave	Ingemark forthcoming
Culbin Sands	Moray	Glass – snake-thread	Stray	Ingemark forthcoming
Mine Howe	Orkney	Glass – snake-thread	Ritual	D Ingemark pers comm
Okstrow	Orkney	Samian	Broch	Hartley 1972, 54

Site	County	Find(s)	Site type	Reference
Westray	Orkney	Glass cup	Burial	Anderson in Davidson 1886, 138-139
Hownam Rings	Roxburgh	Samian	Hillfort	Hartley 1972, 54
Clickhimin	Shetland	Glass painted cup	Broch &c	Hamilton 1968, 138
Scatness	Shetland	Glass painted cup	Broch &c	Turner et al 2002, 386
Leckie	Stirling	Glass cup with snake-thread decoration	Broch	MacKie 2004
Inchgarvie, Queensferry	West Lothian	Denarii of M Aurelius	?(found with other Roman objects)	Curle 1932, 352-353
Crammag Head	Wigtown	Sestertius of Commodus	Broch/dun (casual find close by)	Bateson & Holmes forthcoming
High Torrs	Wigtown	Samian, finger ring	Burial	Breeze & Ritchie 1980
Whithorn	Wigtown	Samian	? (early activity under monastic site)	Dickinson et al 1997, 293

Appendix 2 – late Roman finds, AD 250-400

Italicised entries are from former Roman military sites, and are likely to represent later temporary military reuse rather than native activity. Coin hoards are excluded, as these can be found in Robertson (1978). Stray finds of coins are also excluded, for reasons discussed by Casey (1984); while some will be genuine ancient losses, the detailed autopsy of individual finds has not yet been carried out. The only stray coin plotted in fig 14 is a solidus of Honorius found near the Meikle Loch, Slains, Aberdeenshire around 1876 (Macdonald 1918, 247); archival work by Neil Curtis has indicated this was found during ploughing, and it seems likely to be an ancient loss.

Site	County	Find	Site type	Reference
Kintore	*Aberdeen*	*Coarse ware*	*?reused Roman temporary camp*	*C Wallace pers comm*
Ardnave, Islay	Argyll	Brooch	Hearth in sand dune	Ritchie & Welfare 1983, 341-342
Dun Mor Vaul, Tiree	Argyll	Fine ware	Broch	MacKie 1974, 155, no 3 (identified as LR Oxfordshire ware by C Wallace)
Keil Cave	Argyll	Fine ware	Cave	Ritchie 1967, fig 2.12, 109
Port Sonachan	Argyll	Coarse ware	Stray	Robertson 1964, 200-201 C Wallace, pers comm
Dreghorn	Ayr	Coins (AE)	Uncertain	Robertson 2000, 354, no 1454
Ladykirk	Berwick	Brooch	Stray	Miket 2004, 178, fig 1.10
Crosskirk	Caithness	Fine ware	Broch	Breeze 1984
Keiss Harbour	Caithness	Fine ware	Broch	Curle 1932, 393-394 C Wallace, pers comm
Erickstanebrae	Dumfries	Brooch	Stray	Curle 1932, 370-371 Noll 1974, 227-230
Dumbarton Rock	Dunbarton	Fine ware, coarse ware	Hillfort	Alcock et al 1992
Broxmouth	E Lothian	Bangle	Hillfort	Hill 1982b, 188
Gullane	E Lothian	Coin (AE)	Midden	Younger 1936, 339
Traprain Law	E Lothian	Fine & coarse ware, glass, metalwork, coins, beads, jet, silver hoard	Hillfort	Jobey 1976 for summary
Buittle	Kirkcudbright	Coins (AE)	Open settlement?	Bateson & Holmes 2003, 248
Edinburgh Castle	Midlothian	Fine ware, glass, bracelet	Hillfort	Driscoll & Yeoman 1997, 131-137
Covesea	Moray	Coin hoard (AE), bracelet, beads	Cave	Benton 1931, 191, 199-200, fig 19 no 8 & 10, 209-216

Site	County	Find	Site type	Reference
Bu	Orkney	Antler mounts	Open settlement	Hunter 1993
Howe	Orkney	Glass	Broch	Henderson 1994
Minehowe	Orkney	Fine ware	Ritual & craft	C Wallace, pers comm
Peel	*Perth*	*Coarse ware (identification not certain)*	*Enclosure by Roman signal station*	*Britannia 34 (2003), 302*
Portmahomack	Ross & Cromarty	Coin	Later monastic site	Robertson 1983, 415
Eildon Hill	Roxburgh	Fine ware, coarse ware	Hillfort	Robertson 1970, table VI Dore 1992
Hownam Rings	Roxburgh	Coarse ware	Hillfort	Piggott 1948, 216-217 Robertson 1970, Table VI
Lilliesleaf	Roxburgh	Coin (AE)	Enclosure	Bateson & Holmes 2003, 248
Springwood	Roxburgh	Coins (AE)	Uncertain	Bateson & Holmes 1997, 534; 2003, 248
East Coldoch	Stirling	Glass, beads	Settlement	DES 2004, 129
Carn Liath	Sutherland	Silver brooch*	Broch	Curle 1932, 392 Cessford 1997
Helmsdale	Sutherland	Bronze vessel hoard	Hoard	Spearman 1990
Piltanton Burn	Wigtown	Coins (AE), coarse ware	Uncertain	Bateson & Holmes 2003, 248 C Wallace pers comm
Whithorn	Wigtown	Fine ware, AE coin	? (early activity under monastic site)	Dickinson et al 1997, 293-294, 296
Garry Iochdrach, N Uist	W Isles	Coin (AE)	Wheelhouse	Beveridge & Callander 1932, 41
Udal, N Uist	W Isles	Pot	Wheelhouse	Crawford 2002, 120, 233 (identification not certain; not fully published)
'Moray Firth'	?	Gold crossbow brooch**	Stray	Curle 1932, 392 Kent & Painter 1977, 28 Hartley et al 2006, 168 Tait 1976, 118

* The Carn Liath silver brooch is not a straightforward object. It does not fall readily into conventional Roman brooch typologies, and a number of commentators have suggested it is an indigenous Pictish derivative, even identifying a double-disc symbol on the foot (Cessford 1997; Ritchie 1989, 51). The double-disc is unconvincing to this writer, as similar ring-and-dot motifs are found in various combinations on late Roman brooches; this is true also of the other motifs present, the saltire, geometric edge-notching and peltae[22] (e.g.

Bayley & Butcher 2004, fig 89-91, no 313, 319-321; Hattatt 2000, fig 229 no 505, 1269). The form would seem to indicate a knowledge of late Roman brooches (albeit more like third-century P-shaped ones rather than the fully developed fourth-century crossbows); but the wide range of provincial and barbarian fibulae of the third and fourth centuries needs more careful scrutiny for parallels. At present it is kept here as a late Roman find.

** The provenance of the gold crossbow brooch is frustratingly imprecise, as it appears from the first reference only as 'found on shore of Moray Firth' (Anon 1892, 211, no FE 49). Records in the British Museum indicate it was 'turned up by the plough' in May 1847, and was acquired in 1922 by them from a dealer; it had previously been in the Ashburnham Collection. Unfortunately this provides no real clues to its provenance as the Ashburnhams were a Sussex-based family with wide estates but no obvious connection to Scotland. There appear to be no further records of its provenance in the BM; indeed the 'Moray Firth' provenance was only restored to the original through Robert Stevenson's detective work. I am grateful to Don Bailey, Richard Hobbs and Kenneth Painter for information on its acquisition history.

Appendix 3 – unpublished Roman finds from northern Scotland

This appendix catalogues Roman finds from north of the Forth-Clyde line which have not been properly published. Such stray finds rarely receive full publication, apart from a brief note in *DES*, unless they are particularly striking, but they are a key source of evidence which is too often neglected. Material from excavations is excluded in the expectation that it will be published in due course, although a summary of the material from Birnie is included as it is used heavily in the arguments above. Recent finds from Aberdeenshire are not included, as they will be published elsewhere (Curtis & Hunter in prep). Coins are also excluded, as they are published in regular roundups in the *Proceedings of the Society of Antiquaries of Scotland*. To reduce the risk of unauthorised damage to the findspots, only four-figure grid references are given unless fuller grid references are already published. Full details may be obtained on application to NMS or the museum which holds the object.

It is notable that the material is dominated by brooches. This no doubt partly reflects the source of the evidence, predominantly from metal-detecting. Roman brooches are very recognisable, and it is possible that other Roman material is being recovered but not reported because it is not identified as significant. However, excavated evidence confirms that brooches are by far the predominant type of metal object from native sites, so it seems this is not too great a bias.

NMRS records have been checked for each discovery; unless stated otherwise, no later prehistoric or Roman sites are known in the immediate vicinity of the findspots. All are late first-second century AD in date unless stated. For trumpet brooches, 'types' follow Collingwood & Richmond (1969), while 'groups' follow the classification of Bayley & Butcher (2004, 160-164); the latter is a more meaningful overall classification, but the types still convey subtleties beyond those of the groups where, as is typical of northern Britain, almost all the brooches are of group A.

NORTH-EAST (FORTH-TAY)

St Monance, Fife (fig 22a)
Enamelled headstud brooch. Head and part of bow survive; the brooch has broken at the weakest point of the bow, and is heavily corroded. The riveted headstud is missing, although its oval moulding and rivet hole survive. A crest runs forward from the headstud to the edge of the spring case. The sprung pin is lost; it was once held in a hollow by a fold of metal from the front of the head. The sides of the head bear a champlevé enamel design of a curved blue trumpet design with a bifurcated leaf terminal in a red field. A single blue dot (lost on one side) lies within the concave curve of the trumpet. The design of the decoration and the use of enamelling come from indigenous metalworking traditions, and reflect the fusion of Roman and indigenous styles in the first and early second centuries AD. L 27.5 mm, W 19 mm, H 12 mm. Found by Mr A McAllister in a ploughed field south-west of St Monance while metal-detecting (NGR: NO 521 016; DES 2002, 57). Claimed as Treasure Trove (TT 73/01) and allocated to East Fife Museums Service (CUPMS: 2005.226). Indistinct cropmarks, perhaps from a later prehistoric settlement, are recorded in the same field (NMRS NO 50 SW 458).

Urquhart, Dunfermline, Fife (fig 22b)
Trumpet brooch, undecorated, lacking the spring and foot. Plain knob flanked by mouldings on the bow (present but attenuated on the underside). Integrally-cast loop to hold the lost spring; triangular-sectioned bow with start of flange for catch-plate. Head bent forward from damage; original surface mostly lost. Type R(i); group A. L 36.5 mm, W 14 mm, H 22 mm. Found by Mr S Wilson while metal-detecting (NGR: NT 09 87). Claimed as Treasure Trove (TT 103/05) and allocated to NMS.

Cupar Muir, Fife (fig 22c)
Trumpet brooch, with half-round knob (continued by incised grooves on the underside) flanked by low mouldings of alternating broad and narrow bands.

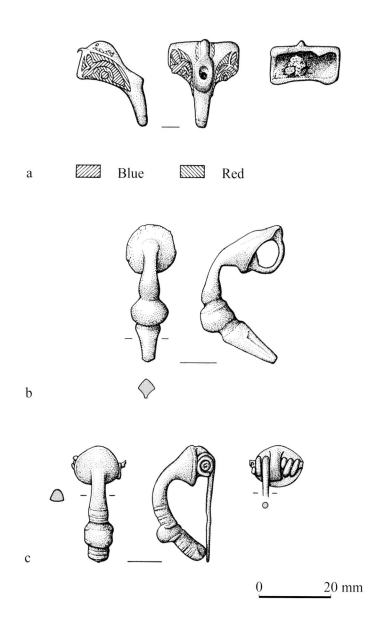

a   ▨ Blue   ▧ Red

b

c

0   20 mm

Fig 22 Recent Roman brooch finds from Fife. (a) St Monance.
(b) Urquhart, Dunfermline. (c) Cupar Muir. Drawn by Marion O'Neil.

The head is plain, with a slightly raised margin. The six-coil spring is held in the integrally-cast lug by a rolled sheet axis; the separate headloop is lost. The pin is intact but the foot of the bow is lost. Group A; type R(iii). L 31 mm, W 15 mm, H 16 mm. Found by Mr J O'Donnell while metal-detecting. NGR: NO 36 13 (another brooch is recorded as coming from this general area: Hunter 1996, 117). Claimed as Treasure Trove (TT 51/98) and allocated to East Fife Museums Service (CUPMS: 2000.0062).

Stirling University, Stirlingshire (fig 23)
Trumpet brooch, lacking most of the catchplate and pin; the stubs of the lug which held the spring survive. The bow knob is a debased acanthus design, encircling the bow. There are possible filemarks from finishing work under the head in one area. Group A; type R(ii). L 44.5 mm; W 10 mm; H 25 mm. Alloy: leaded bronze. NGR: NS 81 96. Found by Mr T H Chalmers while metal-detecting; claimed as Treasure Trove (TT 43/97) and allocated to Stirling Museum (19913).

***Fig 23** Trumpet brooch from Stirling University. © National Museums of Scotland.*

NORTH-EAST (TAY-MORAY FIRTH)

Stoneye, Coupar Angus, Perthshire (fig 24)
Enamelled trumpet brooch in poor condition, with the original surface and

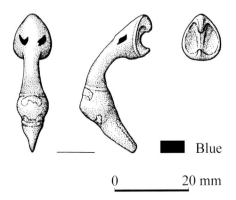

■ Blue

0   20 mm

***Fig 24** Trumpet brooch, Stoneye, Coupar Angus. Drawn by Marion O'Neil.*

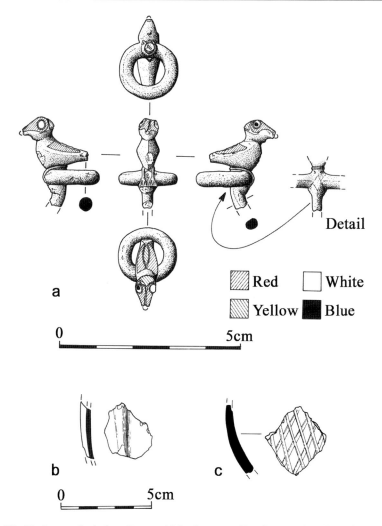

Detail

☑ Red   ☐ White
▩ Yellow ■ Blue

a

0   5cm

b   c

0   5cm

Fig 25 *Roman finds from Birnie. (a) bird mount. (b) pillar-moulded bowl fragment.*
(c) sherd of BB1. Drawn by Alan Braby.

much of the detail lost; the foot and sprung pin are missing. Full acanthus knob, attenuated on the underside. All that survives of the enamelling are two symmetrically-arranged sub-triangular chunks of translucent blue enamel; the design itself is lost. An integral cast lug, now broken, once held the pin. L 37 mm; W 10.5 mm; H 17 mm. Group D; type R(iv). NGR: NO 228 394. Donated to NMS by Mr R Sloan (reg no FT 110). The findspot lies about 2 km north-east of the temporary camp of Lintrose and a few hundred metres south-east of the hypothesised camp at Coupar Angus itself, although the evidence for this latter remains uncertain (RCAHMS 1994, 86). However, given the Roman presence in the vicinity, this brooch may be related to military rather than Iron Age activity in the area.

Birnie

The Roman material from Birnie will be fully published in the final site report, but it is listed in summary and illustrated here (with the exception of the coin hoards) to make the finds more readily available in advance of publication.

Enamelled bird mount, probably a decorative fitting or the ornate head of a projecting ring-headed pin (fig 25a).
Glass vessel: blue glass pillar-moulded bowl fragment of first century date (fig 25b).
Coarse pottery: Black-Burnished Ware jar sherd (BB1) of second century date (fig 25c).
Enamelled disc brooch with projecting lobes (fig 26a).
Trumpet brooch with silver-inlaid decoration (fig 26b).
Variant Alcester-type brooch, with a cylindrical rather than a trumpet head; enamelled, with silvering in areas (fig 26c).
Enamelled tapering bow brooch with three knobs – an unusual type for which no parallels have yet been found (fig 27).

Stonewells, Moray (fig 28a)

Headstud brooch, the hinged pin, catchplate and riveted headstud lost. The wings are decorated with incised transverse lines which bound an enamelled area with a central row of blue diamonds flanked with red triangles. A similar design runs down the bow below the lost headstud, while a raised crest runs from the headstud onto the head. L 37 mm, W 17 mm, H 18 mm. Alloy: gunmetal; blue enamel coloured with cobalt. NGR: NJ 285 659. Found by Mr R Krawczyk while metal-detecting (DES 1999, 26); claimed as Treasure Trove (TT 57/98) and allocated to Elgin Museum (ELGNM 1999.30.2).

Lochhill, Moray (fig 28b)

Enamelled bar brooch, lacking the hinged pin; concavo-convex in profile, the broader convex head with three enamelled strips. The outer strips alternate between turquoise blue and a lost/discoloured colour, the central one orange and a lost colour. The head has two transverse ridges before a plate with three enamelled triangles, now discoloured. A raised knob marks the turning point of the bow; beyond this it tapers to the foot. L 69 mm, W 15 mm, H 25 mm. Alloy: leaded bronze. NGR: NJ 287 650. Found by Mr A McPherson (DES 1999, 64); claimed as Treasure Trove (TT 91/97) and allocated to Elgin Museum (ELGNM 1998.10). NMRS records note ring-ditches and enclosures, perhaps from a settlement, some 200 m to the E (NJ26NE 17).

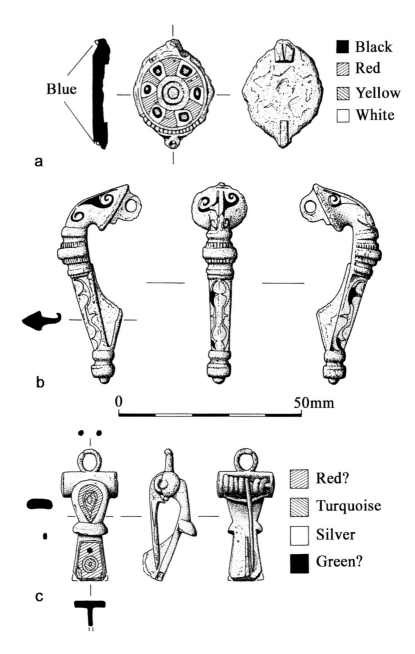

Fig 26 Roman brooches from Birnie. Drawn by Alan Braby.

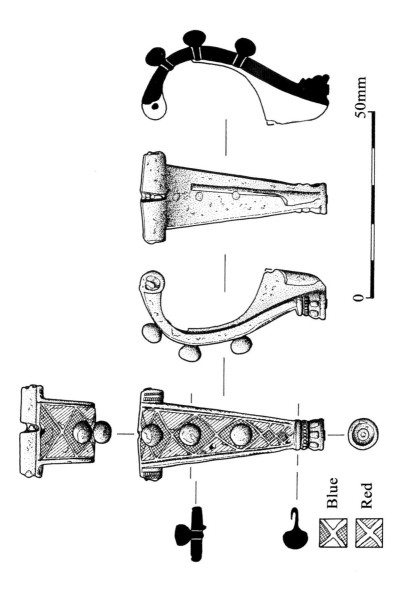

Fig 27 *Roman brooch from Birnie. Drawn by Alan Braby.*

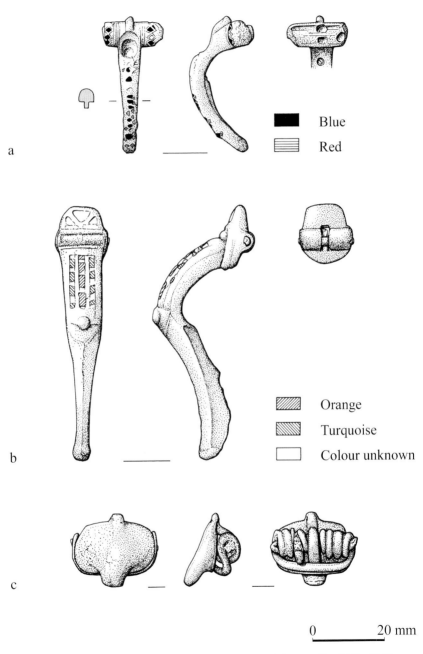

Blue

Red

Orange

Turquoise

Colour unknown

a

b

c

0 _____ 20 mm

Fig 28 *Recent Roman brooch finds from Moray. (a) Stonewells. (b) Lochhill.*
(c) Charlestown, Burghead. Drawn by Marion O'Neil.

This is an example of the 'Wirral' sub-type of bar brooches, a distinctive variant apparently made in north-west England (Philpott 1999): it is of second century AD date. There are five others from Scotland, all from non-Roman contexts: site finds from the hillforts of Traprain Law (E Lothian) and Edinburgh Castle (Midlothian), and stray finds from Pusk (Fife), Peebles (Peeblesshire), and 'the east end of the Antonine Wall'[23] (Burley 1956, no 50; Mackreth 1997, 137; Hunter 1996, 116, ill 2.6; Curle 1932, 368-369; Robertson 1970, 223, fig 10.7). This example is the most northerly findspot of the type.

Charlestown, Burghead, Moray (fig 28c)

Trumpet brooch, only the head surviving; undecorated and flattened from damage. An integrally-cast loop holds an eight-coil spring with internal chord and solid copper alloy axis. A stub of the catch to hold a separate headloop survives. Group A. W 24.5 mm, L 19.5 mm, H 10 mm. NGR: NJ 129 676. Found during metal-detecting by Mr A McPherson; claimed as Treasure Trove (TT 55/05) and allocated to Forres Museum.

The findspot lies some 2.5 km from the Pictish fort at Burghead; it cannot readily be connected to activity there, and thus throws no further light on the question of whether the Pictish fort had a Roman Iron Age precursor. Curle (1932, 296) records a melon bead from the site, supposedly in the National Museum, but there is no trace of this. However the fact that it is recorded by him (and Robertson 1970, 224) as a stray find rather than a site find suggests it has no certain connection to the fort.

Culbin Sands

(fig 29)
Part-melted trumpet brooch, squashed and distorted, with porous and part-melted surfaces, especially on underside. Remains of an acanthus knob flanked by double ribs. Plain head; sprung pin with internal chord and part of chain loop. The bow has been removed below the

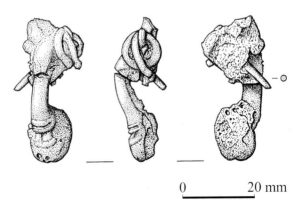

0   20 mm

Fig 29 *Part-melted trumpet brooch, Culbin Sands. Drawn by Marion O'Neil.*

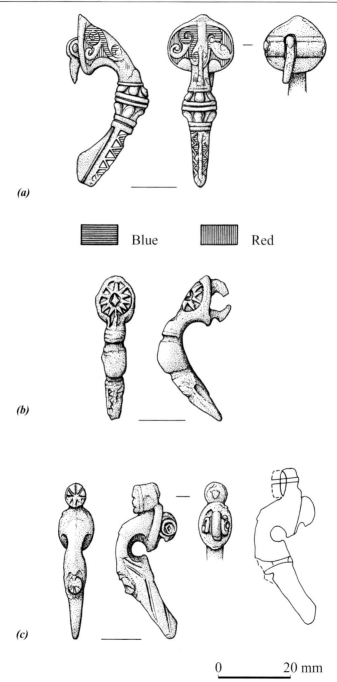

Blue   Red

(a)

(b)

(c)

0 _____ 20 mm

Fig 30 *Trumpet brooches from Achinchanter, Sutherland. Drawn by Marion O'Neil.*

foot, and a crack at the head / bow junction may be from attempts to break off the head. L 38.5 mm, W 17.5 mm, H 14 mm. NMS X.1997.293; an antiquarian find, with no details of find circumstances. NGR: c. NH 98 52.

NORTH SCOTLAND & NORTHERN ISLES

Achinchanter, Sutherland (fig 30)
Enamelled trumpet brooch (fig 30a) with half-round acanthus moulding (highly attenuated rather than flat on the underside). The tip of the foot and much of the catchplate are lost, as is the separate headloop and most of the hinged pin, although the hinge is still held by a solid copper alloy axis through an integrally-cast semi-cylindrical housing with a slot for the pin. The head bears symmetrical red and blue enamel decoration in Celtic style. Each side has an S-spiral in blue with a spiral tendril developed from the larger end in reserved metal, defined by fields of red enamel. Further up the bow the design is too worn to reconstruct, although it may comprise alternating triangles. Below the knob, either side of the bow bears alternating red and blue enamelled triangles. Group D; type R(iv). L 45.5 mm, W (head) 17.5 mm, H 21 mm. Alloy: all components were bronze (minor zinc and lead). Enamels: blue coloured by cobalt, red by copper and lead oxide. NGR: NH 798 904. Found by Mr M Gallon (DES 1995, 47); claimed as Treasure Trove (TT 36/95) and allocated to Inverness Museum (INVMG 1996.006).

Decorated trumpet brooch (fig 30b), lacking the foot, catchplate and sprung pin; the integrally-cast lug to retain the spring is present but broken. Substantial parts of the original surface are lost, and considerable wear on the bow knob complicates precise typological identification. It appears to be a plain half-knob, flanked by triple ridge mouldings (type R(iii)). The head is elaborately decorated: within a circular field a series of marginal triangles, originally no doubt enamelled, define a central 12-pointed star in reserved metal. Within this two chevrons, originally enamelled, define a central diamond. Further channels lead up the bow to the mouldings. The fields are now empty, apart from a single fragment of red enamel. The head is hollowed on the underside to hold the spring, and its edge is worn, but in one area a marginal groove survives on the upper surface. On the bow are the remains of another cast field, largely lost. It comprised a rectangular enamelled field with saw-tooth indents on either side, defining a central spine of reserved diamonds. L 39 mm; W 11 mm; H 20 mm. Alloy: leaded bronze. NGR: NH 796 902. Found by Mr M Gallon (DES 1996, 61); claimed as Treasure Trove (TT 38/97) and allocated to Inverness Museum. (INVMG 1998.002)

Variant trumpet-headed brooch of highly unusual form (fig 30c). The brooch lacks its foot, catchplate and pin, although three turns of the spring and its rolled sheet copper alloy axis are preserved, held by an integrally cast lug. The head is plain apart from a lipped edge and has an integrally-cast solid headloop. A cup-shaped hollow in this bears a decorative iron stud, the head incised with an eight-pointed star defined by simple grooves (stud H 3.5 mm, D 7 mm, overall H 7.5 mm). The bow lacks the knob which is usual on trumpet brooches. Instead it thickens to hold another decorative iron stud with an eight-pointed star, held in a cupped hollow defined by V-grooves on either side. These grooves may originally have held enamel, but corrosion obscures the surface. This feature relates the brooch to the headstud series. Stud dimensions: D 3.5 x 5 mm, overall H 9 mm. The much-worn lower part of the bow, defined by a longitudinal groove on either side, appears to be undecorated.

The overall form is highly unusual: the inner edge of the head curves round towards the bow, which curves out to meet it: the two were originally joined in the casting, with the joining spine subsequently removed. This gives the brooch very much the appearance of a *trompetenmuster* motif (cf MacGregor 1976, 186-188). The edges of this curve are defined by a much-worn raised lip, as are the edges of the central knob. In general the brooch's head relates it to the trumpet form, with influences from the headstud type seen in the bow device; overall it is an unusual interpretation. The similarity to *trompetenmuster* motifs points to a second century AD date. L 42 mm; W 10 mm; H 18 mm. Alloy: (body) leaded bronze; (pin) leaded bronze, lower Zn. NGR: NH 797 903. Found by Mr M Gallon (DES 1996, 61); claimed as Treasure Trove (TT 38/97) and allocated to Inverness Museum (INVMG 1998.001).

The discovery of three Romano-British brooches so far north marks this as an area worthy of further investigation. It may be that its coastal location on the Dornoch Firth gave the area preferential access to Roman goods through trading or exchange networks, like the Culbin Sands in Moray.

South Seatter, Stromness, Orkney (fig 31)

T-shaped bow brooch, lacking pin. T-shaped head, plano-convex in section, with a slight hollow in the centre where the lug to hold the spring broke off. The bow broadens to a poorly-defined knob and then flattens and narrows to the squared foot. The surface is poorly preserved, but the central knob appears to be plain with a single moulding either side. There are remains of tinning in one area. The bow device marks it as a hybrid of the trumpet series, with a variant head. L 43.5 mm, W 22.5 mm, H 21.5 mm. Found during fieldwalking (Richards 2005, 8-16); now in Orkney Museum. NGR: HY 2609 1292.

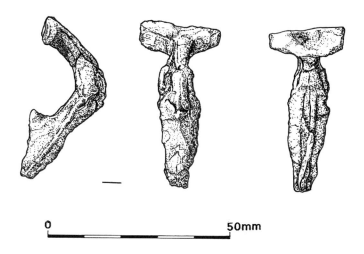

Fig 31 *Roman brooch from South Seatter, Orkney. Drawn by Amanda Brend.*

WESTERN SCOTLAND & WESTERN ISLES

Sound of Flodday, Benbecula (fig 32)
Romano-British penannular brooch, intact, with a good dark green patina consistent with burial in peat. Oval hoop (external D 40 x 36 mm, internal D 33 x 26 mm) formed from a circular-sectioned rod (D 3.5 mm, expanding to 4.5 mm towards the terminals). It is a variant of Fowler (1960) type A3, with knob-and-collar moulding. Here the knobs are plain and flattened with disc terminals (D 5.5 mm); the concave collar is flanked by single shallow circumferential mouldings, while the adjacent hoop bears a design of incised diagonal lines in a zone 7 mm

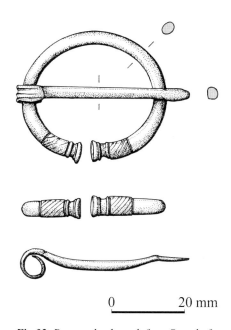

Fig 32 *Penannular brooch from Sound of Flodday, Benbecula. Drawn by Marion O'Neil.*

long, its end defined by a circumferential incised line. The incised designs carry round the rod, although less visible on the inner surface (perhaps from wear), while the collar is absent on the inner surface. The incised lines (spaced about 1 mm apart) are slightly irregular, with overlaps and non-joining segments, suggesting they were incised after casting; the terminals appear to be cast and then reworked slightly.

The intact pin (L 48.5 mm), a rod of D 3 mm, has a low hump and a spade-shaped tip (L 8.5 mm), with two slanting incised lines on the rod just above the tip; these may have been intended to evoke eyes, giving the pin a slightly zoomorphic appearance. The other end is flattened and curled round the hoop, with a slight raised moulding where the curve starts; it is further decorated with two longitudinal channels and, at the rear, an additional central incised line.

Found by Mr Craig Allaker in 2003 while metal-detecting along a stretch of peaty deposit mixed with sand which had been exposed by storm damage. The findspot lies on the north-east corner of Benbecula, about 3 km west of Rosinish; no prehistoric settlement sites are recorded in the area. NGR: NF 849 540. Claimed as Treasure Trove (TT 07/05) and allocated to Museum nan Eilean.

The type does not fit the standard typologies of penannular brooches, but there is little doubt it is a variant of a Romano-British penannular of Fowler type A3. The existing typology classifies only the main types, but considerable variety is known. Many A3 penannulars show some flattening of the knobs (e.g. Keil Cave; Ritchie 1967, fig 2 no 24), and indeed on brooches from Midhowe and Falkirk the inner face is cupped (Callander & Grant 1934, fig 45; unpub, ex inf G Bailey), while zones of incised decoration (circumferential or angled) can be readily paralleled (e.g. on brooches from Fairy Knowe, Stirlingshire and Braithwaite, Cumbria (Hunter 1998, ill 18 no 322; Richardson & Brownsword 1986). The additional effort spent on its manufacture suggests it was in the upper end of the penannular brooch spectrum; this fits the broader picture of Roman brooch use in Iron Age Scotland, where there is a preference for brooches of above-average quality. Fowler gives a date range for the type of first-fourth century AD, but the manufacture of most falls within a late first-second century AD bracket.

Roman finds are not common from the Hebrides, but they are by no means unknown. From Benbecula itself there is a confused antiquarian reference to the discovery of a skeleton along with a hoard of Roman denarii (Robertson 1983, 417), while another Roman brooch was found on either on Benbecula or S Uist (Richardson 1960). Two other brooches are known from settlement sites in South Uist, while samian sherds have come from a number of sites in North Uist and Lewis (Robertson 1970; Hunter 2001). While never present in great quantities, it is clear that Roman finds reached the Hebrides, and it is likely that they were of some value in local power-politics. The ultimate fate of the brooch is also interesting. Its intact condition and discovery in peat-rich soil suggest it was more than a casual loss. A number of personal ornaments are known from peat bogs, and they may represent votive offerings.

Dunan, Skye (fig 33)

Trumpet brooch with full acanthus knob flanked by mouldings. Catchplate broken recently; pin lost in antiquity. Slender bow and head; the bow is triangular-sectioned and plain with side-grooves. The footknob expands but is too badly worn to identify its form. The spring is intact although the pin is lost; it has six coils, and is held by a cast lug. The axis is formed by the wire from the separate headloop (the loop itself largely lost), held by a collar. L 54.5 mm; W (head) 16 mm (knob) 9.5 mm; H 25 mm. Alloy: both brooch and spring are bronze with low levels of zinc and lead; the brooch has a surprisingly high nickel level. Found by Bobby Wildgoose on the beach at Tigh an Dun, Dunan; claimed as Treasure Trove (TT 138/97) and allocated to Skye Museum (1997.1). The place-name suggests there may be a dun in the area, and there is a prominent rocky knoll nearby, although no structural traces survive. NGR: NG 587 281 (DES 1999, 61).

0   20 mm

Fig 33 *Trumpet brooch from Dunan, Skye. Drawn by Marion O'Neil from initial drawings by Steven Birch.*

References

Alcock, L 1963 *Dinas Powys*. Cardiff: University of Wales Press.

Alcock, L 1987 'Pictish studies: present and future', in Small 1987, 80-92.

Alcock, L 2003 *Kings and warriors, craftsmen and priests in northern Britain AD 550-850*. Edinburgh: Society of Antiquaries of Scotland.

Alcock, L & Alcock, E A 1987 'Reconnaissance excavations on Early Historic fortifications and other royal sites in Scotland, 1974-84: 2, Excavations at Dunollie Castle, Oban, Argyll, 1978', *Proc Soc Antiq Scot* 117, 119-147.

Alcock, L & Alcock, E A 1990 'Reconnaissance excavations on Early Historic fortifications and other royal sites in Scotland, 1974-84: 4, Excavations at Alt Clut, Clyde Rock, Strathclyde, 1974-75', *Proc Soc Antiq Scot* 120, 95-149.

Alcock, L, Alcock, E A, Bateson, J D & Webster, P V 1992 'Excavations at Alt Clut, 1974-5: catalogue of coins, metal objects and Romano-British pottery', *Proc Soc Antiq Scot* 122, 289-293.

Alexander, D 2002 'The oblong fort at Finavon, Angus: an example of the over-reliance on the appliance of science?', in Ballin Smith & Banks 2002, 44-54.

Allason-Jones, L 1989 'Small finds of glass and metal', in C Smith, 'Excavations at Dod Law West hillfort, Northumberland', *Northern Archaeology* 9 (1988-9), 23-25.

Allen, D 1944 'The Belgic dynasties of Britain and their coins', *Archaeologia* 90, 1-46.

Anderson, M O 1987 'Picts – the name and the people', in Small 1987, 7-14.

Anon 1892 *Catalogue of the National Museum of Antiquities of Scotland*. Edinburgh: Society of Antiquaries of Scotland.

Armit, I (ed) 1990a *Beyond the brochs: changing perspectives on the Atlantic Scottish Iron Age*. Edinburgh: EUP.

Armit, I 1990b 'Introduction', in Armit 1990a, 1-4.

Armit, I 1990c 'Epilogue', in Armit 1990a, 194-210.

Armit, I 1997a *Celtic Scotland*. London: Batsford / Historic Scotland.

Armit, I 1997b 'Cultural landscapes and identities: a case study in the Scottish Iron Age', in Gwilt and Haselgrove 1997, 248-253.

Armit, I 1999 'The abandonment of souterrains: evolution, catastrophe or dislocation?', *Proc Soc Antiq Scot* 129, 577-596.

Armit, I 2003 *Towers in the north: the brochs of Scotland*. Stroud: Tempus.

Arnold, C J & Davies, J L 2000 *Roman and early Medieval Wales*. Stroud: Sutton.

Ashmore, P J 2004 'Absolute chronology', in I A G Shepherd & G J Barclay (ed), *Scotland in Ancient Europe*, 125-136. Edinburgh: Society of Antiquaries of Scotland.

Atkinson, R J C & Piggott, S 1955 'The Torrs chamfrein', *Archaeologia* 96, 197-235.

Ballin Smith, B 1994 *Howe: four millennia of Orkney prehistory*. Edinburgh: Society of Antiquaries of Scotland.

Ballin Smith, B & Banks, I (ed) 2002 *In the Shadow of the Brochs*. Stroud: Tempus.

Barrow, G W S 1989 'The tribes of north Britain revisited', *Proc Soc Antiq Scot* 119, 161-163.

Bateson, J D & Holmes, N M McQ 1997 'Roman and medieval coins found in Scotland, 1988-95', *Proc Soc Antiq Scot* 127, 527-561.

Bateson, J D & Holmes, N M McQ 2003 'Roman and medieval coins found in Scotland, 1996-2000', *Proc Soc Antiq Scot* 133, 245-276.

Bateson, J D & Holmes, N M McQ forthcoming 'Roman and medieval coins found in Scotland, 2001-5', *Proc Soc Antiq Scot*.

Bayley, J & Butcher, S 2004 *Roman brooches in Britain: a technological and typological study based on the Richborough collection*. London: Society of Antiquaries of London.

Bélier, A-C 1982 'A sherd of terra sigillata from Wood Quay, Dublin', *Ulster J Archaeol* 44-5 (1981-2), 192-194.

Benton, S 1931 'The excavation of the Sculptor's Cave, Covesea, Morayshire', *Proc Soc Antiq Scot* 65 (1930-31), 177-216.

Berger, F 1996 'Roman coins beyond the northern frontiers: some recent considerations', in C E King & D G Wigg (ed), *Coin finds and coin use in the Roman world*, 55-61. Berlin: Mann Verlag.

Besteman, J C, Bos, J M, Gerrets, D A, Heidinga, H A & de Koning, J 1999 *The excavations at Wijnaldum Volume 1*. Rotterdam: A A Balkema.

Beveridge, E & Callander, J G 1932 'Earth-houses at Garry Iochdrach and Bac Mhic Connain, in North Uist', *Proc Soc Antiq Scot* 66 (1931-2), 32-66.

Billingsley, J 1998 *Stony gaze: investigating Celtic and other stone heads*. Chieveley: Capall Bann Publishing.

Birley A 1988 *The African emperor: Septimius Severus*. London: Batsford.

Birley, A 2001 'The Anavionenses', in N J Higham (ed), *Archaeology of the Roman Empire: a tribute to the life and works of Professor Barri Jones*, 15-24. Oxford: BAR.

Boon, G C 1994 'Mould for false *denarii*', in D Maynard, 'Archaeological discoveries in the dune system at Brighouse Bay', *Trans Dumfries Galloway Nat Hist Antiq Soc* 69, 13-33 (21).

Bradley, J 1982 ' 'Medieval' samian ware – a medicinal suggestion', *Ulster J Archaeol* 44-5 (1981-2), 196-197.

Breeze, D J 1982 *The northern frontiers of Roman Britain*. London: Batsford.

Breeze, D J 1984 'The potsherd of Castor Ware from Crosskirk' in H Fairhurst, *Excavations at Crosskirk broch, Caithness*, 115. Edinburgh: Society of Antiquaries of Scotland.

Breeze, D J 1994 'The imperial legacy – Rome and her neighbours', in Crawford 1994, 1-19.

Breeze, D J 1997 'The Great Myth of Caledon', in T C Smout (ed), *Scottish Woodland History*, 47-51. Edinburgh: Scottish Cultural Press.

Breeze, D J 2003 'Warfare in Britain and the building of Hadrian's Wall', *Arch Aeliana* (fifth series) 32, 13-16.

Breeze, D J & Ritchie, J N G 1980 'A Roman burial at High Torrs, Luce Sands, Wigtownshire', *Trans Dumfries Galloway Nat Hist Antiq Soc* 55, 77-85.

Burley, E 1956 'A catalogue and survey of the metal-work from Traprain Law', *Proc Soc Antiq Scot* 89 (1955-6), 118-226.

Callander, J G & Grant, W G 1934 'The broch of Midhowe, Rousay, Orkney', *Proc Soc Antiq Scot* 68 (1933-34), 444-516.

Cambridge, O & Watt, T 2003 'The northernmost Roman brooch from Britain', *Lucerna* 26, 8.

Carroll, M 2002 'Measuring time and inventing histories in the early Empire: Roman and Germanic perspectives', in M Carruthers, C van Driel-Murray, A Gardner, J Lucas, L Revell & E Swift (ed), *TRAC 2001: Proceedings of the eleventh annual Theoretical Roman Archaeology Conference Glasgow 2001*, 104-112. Oxford: Oxbow.

Casey, J 1984 'Roman coinage of the fourth century in Scotland', in R Miket & C Burgess (ed), *Between and Beyond the Walls*, 295-304. Edinburgh: John Donald.

Cessford, C 1997 'The crossbow brooch from Carn Liath', *Pictish Arts Soc J* 11, 19-22.

Childe, V G 1935 *The prehistory of Scotland*. London: Kegan Paul.

Close-Brooks, J 1986 'Excavations at Clatchard Craig, Fife', *Proc Soc Antiq Scot* 116, 117-184.

Coleman, R & Hunter, F 2002 'The excavation of a souterrain at Shanzie Farm, Alyth, Perthshire', *Tayside & Fife Archaeol J* 8, 77-101.

Collingwood, R G & Richmond, I A 1969 *The archaeology of Roman Britain*. London: Methuen.

Cool, H E M 2000 'The parts left over: material culture in the fifth century', in T Wilmott & P Wilson (ed), *The late Roman transition in the north*, 47-65. Oxford: BAR.

Cowie, T G 1986 'A stone head from Port Appin, Argyll', *Proc Soc Antiq Scot* 116, 89-91.

Crawford, B E (ed) 1994 *Scotland in Dark Age Europe*. St Andrews: Committee for Dark Age Studies, University of St Andrews.

Crawford, I 2002 'The wheelhouse', in Ballin Smith & Banks 2002, 111-128.

Cree, J E 1923 'Account of the excavations on Traprain Law during the summer of 1922', *Proc Soc Antiq Scot* 57 (1922-23), 180-226.

Crone, A 2000 *The history of a Scottish lowland crannog: excavations at Buiston, Ayrshire, 1989-90.* Edinburgh: STAR.

Cunliffe, B 2001 *The extraordinary voyage of Pytheas the Greek.* London: Allen Lane.

Cunliffe, B 2005 *Iron Age communities in Britain* (fourth edition). London: Routledge.

Curle, A O 1915 'Account of excavations on Traprain Law in the parish of Prestonkirk, county of Haddington in 1914', *Proc Soc Antiq Scot* 49 (1914-15), 139-202.

Curle, A O 1923 *The Treasure of Traprain.* Glasgow: Maclehose.

Curle, A O & Cree, J E 1916 'Account of excavations on Traprain Law in the parish of Prestonkirk, county of Haddington, in 1915', *Proc Soc Antiq Scot* 50 (1915-16), 64-144.

Curle, J 1911 *A Roman Frontier Post and its People: the fort of Newstead in the parish of Melrose.* Glasgow: Maclehose.

Curle, J 1932 'An inventory of objects of Roman and provincial Roman origin found on sites in Scotland not definitely associated with Roman constructions', *Proc Soc Antiq Scot* 66 (1931-2), 277-397.

Curtis, N G W & Hunter, F in prep 'Two Roman bronze vessels from Stoneywood, Aberdeen', for submission to *Proc Soc Antiq Scot.*

Dalwood, C H, Buteux, V A & Jackson, R A 1992 'Interim report on excavations at Deansway, Worcester 1988-1989', *Trans Worcester Archaeol Soc* (third series) 13, 121-128.

Davidson, J 1886 'Notice of a small cup-shaped glass vessel, found in a stone cist at the public school, Airlie…', *Proc Soc Antiq Scot* 20 (1885-6), 136-141.

De Micheli, C 1992 'A bronze bowl of Irchester type from Stainfield, Lincolnshire', *Britannia* 23, 238-241.

DES *Discovery and Excavation in Scotland.* Edinburgh: Council for Scottish Archaeology.

Deyts, S 2002 'Les débuts de la statuaire en Gaule centrale', in D Maranski & V Guichard (ed), *Les âges du Fer en Nivernais, Bourbonnais et Berry oriental. Regards européens sur les âges du Fer en France*, 267-270. Glux-en-Glenne: Collections Bibracte.

Dickinson, B, Hill, P, Holmes, N, Millett, M & Price, J 1997 'The Roman finds' in P Hill, *Whithorn and St Ninian: the excavation of a monastic town, 1984-91*, 292-297. Stroud: Whithorn Trust.

Dodds, W 1978 'A Celtic head from Rose Hall, Trohoughton, Dumfries', *Trans Dumfries Galloway Nat Hist Antiq Soc* 53 (1977-8), 182-183.

Dore, J N 1992 'Roman pottery', in J S Rideout, O A Owen & E Halpin, *Hillforts of southern Scotland*, 47-48. Edinburgh: STAR.

Driscoll, S T & Yeoman, P A 1997 *Excavations within Edinburgh Castle in 1988-91*. Edinburgh: Society of Antiquaries of Scotland.

Dungworth, D B 1996 'The production of copper alloys in Iron Age Britain', *Proc Prehist Soc* 62, 399-421.

Earwood, C 1993 *Domestic wooden artefacts in Britain and Ireland from Neolithic to Viking times*. Exeter: University of Exeter Press.

Edwards, K J & Ralston, I B M 2003 *Scotland after the Ice Age: Environment, Archaeology and History 8000 BC – AD 1000*. Edinburgh: EUP.

Eggers, H J 1951 *Der römische Import im freien Germanien*. Hamburg: Hamburgisches Museum für Völkerkunde und Vorgeschichte.

Erdrich, M 1999 'Continuity or discontinuity: native and Roman metal finds', in Besteman et al 1999, 171-183.

Erdrich, M 2000 *Rom und die Barbaren: Das Verhältnis zwischen dem Imperium Romanum und den Germanischen Stämmen vor seiner Nordwestgrenze von der späten römischen Republik bis zum Galischen Sonderreich*. Mainz: Römisch-Germanische Kommission.

Erdrich, M, Giannotta, K M & Hanson, W S 2000 'Traprain Law: native and Roman on the northern frontier', *Proc Soc Antiq Scot* 130, 441-456.

Feachem, R W 1966 'The hill-forts of northern Britain', in A L F Rivet (ed) *The Iron Age in Northern Britain*, 59-87. Edinburgh: EUP.

Fitts, L 1998 '*Inde opes et rerum secundarum luxus*, Stanwick and Melsonby', in J Bird (ed), *Form and Fabric: studies in Rome's material past in honour of B. R. Hartley*, 1-7. Oxford: Oxbow.

Fitts, R L, Haselgrove, C C, Lowther, P C & Willis, S H 1999 'Melsonby revisited: survey and excavation 1992-95 at the site of discovery of the "Stanwick", North Yorkshire, hoard of 1843', *Durham Archaeol J* 14-15, 1-52.

Fitzpatrick, A P 1989 'The submission of the Orkney Islands to Claudius: new evidence?', *Scottish Archaeol Rev* 6, 24-33.

Fitzpatrick, A P 2003 'The place of Gaulish wine in the military supply of amphorae-borne commodities in Roman Scotland', *J Roman Pottery Studies* 10, 60-63.

Fitzpatrick, A P forthcoming 'Dancing with dragons: fantastic animals in the earlier Celtic art of Iron Age Britain', in Haselgrove & Moore forthcoming.

Ford, B 2003 'Coarse pottery' in Holmes 2003, 58-86.

Foster, S M 1990 'Pins, combs and the chronology of later Atlantic Iron Age settlement', in Armit 1990a, 143-174.

Foster, S M 1998 'Before *Alba*: Pictish and Dál Riata power centres from the fifth to the late ninth centuries AD', in S Foster, A Macinnes & R Macinnes (ed), *Scottish Power Centres from the Early Middle Ages to the Twentieth Century*, 1-31. Glasgow: Cruithne Press.

Foster, S M 2004 *Picts, Gaels and Scots*. London: Batsford / Historic Scotland.

Fowler, E 1960 'The origins and development of the penannular brooch in Europe', *Proc Prehist Soc* 26, 149-177.

Fraser, J E 2005 *The Roman conquest of Scotland: the battle of Mons Graupius AD 84*. Stroud: Tempus.

Frere, S S 1991 *Britannia: a history of Roman Britain* (third edition). London: Pimlico.

Frey, O-H 2000 'Keltische Großplastik', *Reallexikon der Germanischen Altertumskunde* 16, 395-407. Berlin: Walter de Gruyter.

Friell, J G P & Watson, W G (ed) 1984 *Pictish Studies: settlement, burial and art in Dark Age northern Britain*. Oxford: BAR.

Galestin, M C 1999 'Roman wheelthrown pottery, terra nigra-like bowls and tiles', in Besteman et al 1999, 157-169.

Gentles, D 1993 'Vitrified forts', *Current Archaeology* 133, 18-20.

Going, C J 1992 'Economic 'long waves' in the Roman period? A reconnaissance of the Romano-British ceramic evidence', *Oxford J Archaeol* 11/1, 93-117.

Gomez de Soto, J & Milcent, P-Y 2002 'La sculpture de l'âge du Fer en France centrale et occidentale', *Documents d'Archéologie Méridionale* 25, 261-267.

Gordon, A 1726 *Itinerarium Septentrionale*. London: privately published.

Goudineau, C 1998 'Les Gaulois: ont-ils représenté leurs dieux? De Glauberg à Roquepertuse', in S Deyts (ed), *À la recontre des Dieux gaulois: un défi à César*, 20-23. Lattes: Musée Archéologique Henri Prades.

Grimme, E G 1968 *Große Kunst aus tausend Jahren: Kirchenschätze aus dem Bistum Aachen*. Düsseldorf: Verlag L Schwann (=Aachener Kunstblätter 36).

Guido, M 1978 *The glass beads of the prehistoric and Roman periods in Britain and Ireland*. London: Society of Antiquaries of London (Research Report 35).

Gwilt, A & Haselgrove, C (ed) 1997 *Reconstructing Iron Age Societies*. Oxford: Oxbow.

Hamilton, J R C 1968 *Excavations at Clickhimin, Shetland*. Edinburgh: HMSO.

Hanson, W S 2003 'The Roman presence: brief interludes', in Edwards & Ralston 2003, 195-216.

Hanson, W S forthcoming *The Roman fort of Elginhaugh*. London: Roman Society.

Hanson, W S & Maxwell, G S 1983 *Rome's north west frontier: the Antonine Wall*. Edinburgh: EUP.

Harding, D W (ed) 1982 *Later prehistoric settlement in south-east Scotland*. Edinburgh: University of Edinburgh Dept of Archaeology.

Harding, D W 2004 *The Iron Age in northern Britain*. London: Routledge.

Harding, D W & Dixon, T N 2000 *Dun Bharabhat, Cnip: an Iron Age settlement in West Lewis. Volume 1: the structures and material culture.* Edinburgh: University of Edinburgh Dept of Archaeology.

Hartley, B R 1972 'The Roman occupations of Scotland: the evidence of samian ware', *Britannia* 3, 1-55.

Hartley, B 1997 'Samian ware and other Roman fine wares', in Driscoll & Yeoman 1997, 133-134.

Hartley, E, Hawkes, J, Henig, M & Mee, F 2006 *Constantine the Great: York's Roman Emperor.* York: York Museums & Gallery Trust.

Hartley, K 2003 'Mortaria', in Holmes 2003, 49-58.

Haselgrove, C 1979 'The significance of coinage in pre-Conquest Britain', in B C Burnham & H C Johnson (ed), *Invasion and Response: the case of Roman Britain*, 197-209. Oxford: BAR.

Haselgrove, C 1984 '"Romanization" before the conquest: Gaulish precedents and British consequences', in T F C Blagg & A C King (ed), *Military and Civilian in Roman Britain*, 5-63. Oxford: BAR.

Haselgrove, C & Moore, T forthcoming *The later Iron Age of Britain and the near Continent.* Oxford: Oxbow.

Hattatt, R 2000 *A visual catalogue of Richard Hattatt's ancient brooches.* Oxford: Oxbow.

Heald, A 2001 'Knobbed spearbutts of the British and Irish Iron Age: new examples and new thoughts', *Antiquity* 75, 689-696.

Heald, A 2005 *Non-ferrous metalworking in Iron Age Scotland 700 BC – AD 700.* Unpublished PhD thesis, Edinburgh University.

Heather, P 1994 'State formation in Europe in the first millennium AD', in Crawford 1994, 47-70.

Helander, A 1997 'Ett Terra Sigillata-kärl i Linköping – det hittills nordligaste fyndet', *Fornvännen* 92, 49-56.

Henderson, J 1994 'The glass', in Ballin Smith 1994, 234-236.

Henderson, J & Kemp, M M B 1992 'Glass', in J S Rideout, O A Owen & E Halpin, *Hillforts of southern Scotland*, 42-45. Edinburgh: STAR.

Henig, M 1978 *A corpus of Roman engraved gemstones from British sites.* Oxford: BAR.

Henig, M 2000 *English gem-set seals.* Stoke-on-Trent: Finds Research Group (Datasheet 27).

Hicks, C 1993 'The Pictish Class I animals', in Spearman and Higgitt 1993, 196-202.

Hill, P H 1982a 'Settlement and chronology', in Harding 1982, 4-43.

Hill, P H 1982b 'Broxmouth hillfort excavations, 1977-1978: an interim report', in Harding 1982, 141-188.

Hind, J G F 1983 'Caledonia and its occupation under the Flavians', *Proc Soc Antiq Scot* 113, 373-378.

Hingley, R 1992 'Society in Scotland from 700 BC to AD 200', *Proc Soc Antiq Scot* 122, 7-53.

Hogg, A H A 1945 'Roman fragments from Castle Dykes near Cockburnspath and from St Abb's Head', *Proc Soc Antiq Scot* 79 (1944-5), 172-173.

Holmes, N 2003 *Excavation of Roman sites at Cramond, Edinburgh.* Edinburgh: Society of Antiquaries of Scotland.

Holmes, N M McQ 2004 'Roman coin', in D D A Simpson, R A Gregory & E M Murphy, 'Excavations at Kaimes Hill, Ratho, City of Edinburgh, 1964-72', *Proc Soc Antiq Scot* 134, 65-118 (104-105).

Holmes, N M McQ 2006 'Two denarius hoards from Birnie, Moray', *British Numismatic Journal 76,1-44.*

Holmes, N & Hunter, F 2001 'Roman counterfeiters' moulds from Scotland', *Proc Soc Antiq Scot* 131, 167-176.

Horn, H G 1989 'Si per me misit, nil nisi vota feret. Ein römischer Spielturm aus Froitzheim', *Bonner J* 189, 139-160.

Horsnæs, H W 2003 'The coins in the bogs' in Jørgensen et al 2003, 330-340.

Hunter, F 1993 'Four decorated antler mounts and a stone 'egg' amulet from Bu Sands, Burray, Orkney', *Proc Soc Antiq Scot* 123, 319-336.

Hunter, F 1996 'Recent Roman Iron Age metalwork finds from Fife and Tayside', *Tayside & Fife Archaeol J* 2, 113-125.

Hunter, F 1997 'Iron Age hoarding in Scotland and northern England', in Gwilt & Haselgrove 1997, 108-133.

Hunter, F 1998 'Copper alloy' in Main 1998, 338-346.

Hunter, F 2001 'Roman and native in Scotland: new approaches', *J Roman Archaeology* 14, 289-309.

Hunter, F 2002 'Problems in the study of Roman and native' in P Freeman, J Bennett, Z T Fiema & B Hoffmann (ed), *Limes XVIII: Proceedings of the XVIIIth International Congress of Roman Frontier Studies held in Amman, Jordan (September 2000)*, 43-50. Oxford: BAR.

Hunter, F 2005 'Rome and the creation of the Picts', in Z Visy (ed), *Limes XIX: Proceedings of the XIXth International Congress of Roman Frontier Studies held in Pécs, Hungary, September 2003*, 235-244. Pécs: University of Pécs.

Hunter, F forthcoming a 'Silver for the barbarians: interpreting denarii hoards in north Britain and beyond', in R Hingley & S Willis (ed), *Roman finds: context and theory.* Oxford: Oxbow.

Hunter, F forthcoming b 'Artefacts, regions and identities in the northern British Iron Age', in Haselgrove & Moore forthcoming.

Hunter, F forthcoming c 'New light on Iron Age massive armlets', *Proc Soc Antiq Scot.*

Ingemark, D 2003 *Glass, alcohol and power in Roman Iron Age Scotland.* Unpublished PhD dissertation, Lund University.

Ingemark, D 2005 'Roman glass', in D Alexander, 'Redcastle, Lunan Bay, Angus: the excavation of an Iron Age timber-lined souterrain and a Pictish barrow cemetery', *Proc Soc Antiq Scot* 135, 41-118 (80-82).

Ingemark, D forthcoming *Glass, alcohol and power in Roman Iron Age Scotland*. Edinburgh: NMS.

Ireland, S 1986 *Roman Britain: a sourcebook*. London: Routledge.

Jackson, K H 1969 *The Gododdin: the oldest Scottish poem*. Edinburgh: EUP.

Jobey, G 1976 'Traprain Law: a summary', in D W Harding (ed), *Hillforts*, 191-204. London: Academic Press.

Jobey, G 1978 'Burnswark Hill, Dumfriesshire', *Trans Dumfries Galloway Nat Hist Antiq Soc* 53 (1977-8), 57-104.

Johns, C 2003 'Romano-British sculpture: intention and execution', in P Noelke (ed), *Romanisation und Resistenz in Plastik, Architektur und Inschriften der Provinzen des Imperium Romanum*, 27-38. Mainz: von Zabern.

Jones, B, Keillar, I & Maude, K 1993 'The Moray aerial survey: discovering the prehistoric and protohistoric landscape', in W D H Sellar (ed), *Moray: Province and People*, 47-74. Edinburgh: Scottish Society for Northern Studies.

Jørgensen, L, Storgaard, B & Thomsen, L G 2003 *The spoils of victory: the north in the shadow of the Roman Empire*. Copenhagen: Nationalmuseet.

Kennett, D H 1968 'The Irchester bowls', *J Northampton Museum & Art Gallery* 4, 5-39.

Kent, J P C & Painter, K S (ed) 1977 *Wealth of the Roman World AD 300-700*. London: British Museum.

Keppie, L 1989 'Beyond the northern frontier: Roman and native in Scotland', in M Todd (ed), *Research on Roman Britain: 1960-89*, 61-73. London: Society for the Promotion of Roman Studies.

Kilbride-Jones, H E 1980 *Celtic Craftsmanship in Bronze*. London: Croom Helm.

Koch, J T 1980 'The stone of the *Weni-kones*', *Bulletin Board Celtic Studies* 29/1, 87-89.

Kornbluth, G A 1989 'The Alfred Jewel: reuse of Roman *spolia*', *Medieval Arch* 33, 32-37.

Laing, L 1975 *The archaeology of late Celtic Britain and Ireland*. London: Methuen.

Laing, L & Laing, J 1984 'The date and origin of the Pictish symbols', *Proc Soc Antiq Scot* 114, 261-276.

Laing, L & Laing, J 1986 'Scottish and Irish metalwork and the '*conspiratio barbarica*'', *Proc Soc Antiq Scot* 116, 211-221.

Lane, A & Campbell, E 2000 *Dunadd: an early Dalriadic capital*. Oxford: Oxbow.

Lind, L 1981 *Roman denarii found in Sweden 2. Catalogue text*. Stockholm: Almqvist & Wiksell.

Lund Hansen, U 1987 *Römischer Import im Norden*. Copenhagen: Det Kongelike Nordiske Oldskriftselskab.

Macdonald, G 1918 'Roman coins found in Scotland', *Proc Soc Antiq Scot* 52 (1917-18), 203-276.

MacGregor, M 1976 *Early Celtic Art in North Britain*. Leicester: Leicester University Press.

Macinnes, L 1982 'Pattern and purpose: the settlement evidence', in Harding 1982, 57-73.

Macinnes, L 1984 'Brochs and the Roman occupation of lowland Scotland', *Proc Soc Antiq Scot* 114, 235-249.

Macinnes, L 1989 'Baubles, bangles and beads: trade and exchange in Roman Scotland', in J Barrett, A P Fitzpatrick & L Macinnes (ed), *Barbarians and Romans in North-West Europe*, 108-116. Oxford: BAR.

MacKie, E W 1974 *Dun Mor Vaul: an Iron Age broch on Tiree*. Glasgow: University of Glasgow Press.

MacKie, E W 2004 'More remarkable Roman objects from Leckie broch, Stirlingshire – part II', *Glasgow Archaeol Soc Newsletter* 53.

Mackreth, D 1997 'Roman period brooches and other bronzework' in Driscoll & Yeoman 1997, 136-138.

Main, L 1998 'Excavation of a timber round-house and broch at the Fairy Knowe, Buchlyvie, Stirlingshire, 1975-8', *Proc Soc Antiq Scot* 128, 293-417.

Malden, J 2000 'Archaeological overview: the discovery of the drain', in J Malden (ed), *The monastery and abbey of Paisley*, 173-180. Glasgow: Renfrewshire Local History Forum.

Mann, J 1974 'The northern frontier after AD 369', *Glasgow Archaeol J* 3, 34-42.

Mann, J C & Breeze, D J 1987 'Ptolemy, Tacitus and the tribes of north Britain', *Proc Soc Antiq Scot* 117, 85-91.

Maxwell, G S 1983 'Recent aerial survey in Scotland', in G S Maxwell (ed), *The impact of aerial reconnaissance on archaeology*, 27-40. York: CBA.

Maxwell, G S 1987 'Settlement in southern Pictland: a new overview', in Small 1987, 31-44.

Maxwell, G 1990 *A Battle Lost: Romans and Caledonians at Mons Graupius*. Edinburgh: EUP.

Maxwell, G 1998 *A gathering of eagles: scenes from Roman Scotland*. Edinburgh: Canongate / Historic Scotland.

Maxwell, S 1951 'Discoveries made in 1934 on King Fergus' Isle and elsewhere in Loch Laggan, Inverness-shire', *Proc Soc Antiq Scot* 85 (1950-51), 160-165.

Megaw, J V S 1970 'Cheshire Cat and Mickey Mouse: analysis, interpretation and the art of the La Tène Iron Age', *Proc Prehist Soc* 36, 261-279.

Ménez, Y 1999 'Les sculptures gauloises de Paule (Côtes-d'Armor)', *Gallia* 56, 357-414.

Miket, R 2002 'The souterrains of Skye', in Ballin Smith & Banks 2002, 77-110.

Miket, R 2004 'Archaeological finds from the Tweed valley in 2002-3', *Archaeologia Aeliana* (fifth series) 33, 175-181.

Miller, M 1975 'Stilicho's Pictish War', *Britannia* 6, 141-145.

Morris, R W B & van Hoek, M A M 1987 'Rock carvings in the Garlieston area, Wigtown district', *Trans Dumfries Galloway Nat Hist Antiq Soc* 62, 32-39.

Murray, H J R 1951 *A history of board-games other than chess*. Oxford: Clarendon Press.

Nash, D 1978 *Settlement and coinage in central Gaul c. 200-50 B.C.* Oxford: BAR.

Nieke, M R 1993 'Penannular and related brooches: secular ornament or symbol in action?', in Spearman & Higgitt 1993, 128-134.

Nielsen, S 1988 'Roman denarii in Denmark – an archaeological approach', *Nordisk Numismatisk Årsskrift* 1987-8, 147-169.

Noll, R 1974 'Eine goldene 'Kaiserfibel' aus Niederemmel vom Jahre 316', *Bonner Jahrbücher* 174, 221-244.

Olivier, L 2003 'La Dame de Beaupréau (Maine-et-Loire): une nouvelle statue gauloise au torque du IIe siècle av. J.-C.', *Antiquités Nationales* 35, 13-17.

Petersen, P V 2003 'Warrior art, religion and symbolism', in Jørgensen et al 2003, 286-294.

Petit, C & Wahlen, P 2005 'Une statue gauloise découverte sur le sanctuaire de Molesme (Côte-d'Or, France)', *Archäologisches Korrespondenzblatt* 35, 223-232.

Philpott, R 1999 'A Romano-British brooch type from north-western and northern England', *Britannia* 30, 274-286.

Piggott, C M 1948 'The excavations at Hownam Rings, Roxburghshire, 1948', *Proc Soc Antiq Scot* 82 (1947-8), 193-225.

Piggott, S 1953 'Three metal-work hoards of the Roman period from southern Scotland', *Proc Soc Antiq Scot* 87 (1952-3), 1-50.

Price, J & Cottam, S 1998 *Romano-British glass vessels: a handbook*. York: CBA.

Proudfoot, E 1996 'Excavations at the long cist cemetery on the Hallow Hill, St Andrews, Fife, 1975-7', *Proc Soc Antiq Scot* 126, 387-454.

Raftery, B 2005 'Ireland and Scotland in the Iron Age', in W Gillies & D W Harding (ed), *Celtic Connections Volume 2: archaeology, numismatics and historical linguistics*, 181-189. Edinburgh: University of Edinburgh Archaeology Monograph Series 2.

Ralston, I B M 1979 'The Iron Age: Northern Britain', in J V S Megaw & D D A Simpson (ed), *Introduction to British Prehistory*, 446-501. Leicester: Leicester University Press.

Ralston, I 1987 'Portknockie: promontory forts and Pictish settlement in the North-East', in Small 1987, 15-26.

Ralston, I 2004 *The hill-forts of Pictland since 'The Problem of the Picts'*. Rosemarkie: Groam House.

Ralston, I, Sabine, K & Watt, W 1983 'Later prehistoric settlements in north-east Scotland: a preliminary assessment' in J C Chapman & H C Mytum (ed), *Settlement in North Britain 1000 BC – AD 1000*, 149-173. Oxford: BAR.

RCAHMS 1994 *South-east Perth: an archaeological landscape*. Edinburgh: RCAHMS.

RIB I   Collingwood, R G & Wright, R P 1965 *The Roman Inscriptions of Britain I. Inscriptions on stone*. Oxford: OUP.

RIB II   Collingwood, R G & Wright, R P *The Roman Inscriptions of Britain II. Instrumentum Domesticum,* (ed S S Frere & R S O Tomlin). Stroud: Alan Sutton.

Richards, C (ed) 2005 *Dwelling among the monuments*. Cambridge: Macdonald Institute.

Richardson, C & Brownsword, R 1986 'A Roman brooch from Braithwaite, Cumbria', *Trans Cumb Westmorland Arch Antiq Soc* (second series) 86, 264-266.

Richardson, K M 1960 'A Roman brooch from the Outer Hebrides, with notes on others of its type', *Antiq J* 40, 200-213.

Richmond, I A 1961 'Ancient geographical sources for Britain north of Cheviot', in I A Richmond (ed) *Roman and native in north Britain*, 131-155. Edinburgh: Thomas Nelson.

Ritchie, A 1984 'The archaeology of the Picts: some current problems', in Friell & Watson 1984, 1-6.

Ritchie, A 1989 *Picts*. Edinburgh: HMSO.

Ritchie, J N G 1967 'Keil Cave, Southend, Argyll: a late Iron Age cave occupation in Kintyre', *Proc Soc Antiq Scot* 99 (1966-7), 104-110.

Ritchie, G & Welfare, H 1983 'Excavations at Ardnave, Islay', *Proc Soc Antiq Scot* 113, 302-366.

Rivet, A L F & Smith, C 1979 *The place-names of Roman Britain*. London: Batsford.

Robertson, A S 1964 'Miscellanea Romano-Caledonica', *Proc Soc Antiq Scot* 97 (1963-4), 180-201.

Robertson, A 1970 'Roman finds from non-Roman sites in Scotland', *Britannia* 1, 198-226.

Robertson, A S 1971 'Roman coins found in Scotland, 1961-70', *Proc Soc Antiq Scot* 103 (1970-1), 113-168.

Robertson, A S 1978 'The circulation of Roman coins in north Britain: the evidence of hoards and site-finds from Scotland', in R A G Carson & C M Kraay (ed), *Scripta Nummaria Romana: essays presented to Humphrey Sutherland*, 186-216. London: Spink.

Robertson, A S 1983 'Roman coins found in Scotland, 1971-82', *Proc Soc Antiq Scot* 113, 405-448.

Robertson, A S 1993 'Finds of Imperial Roman coins in Britain from Near-Eastern and Eastern mints: the evidence of Romano-British coin hoards', in M Price, A Burnett & R Bland (ed), *Essays in honour of Robert Carson and Kenneth Jenkins*, 229-240. London: Spink.

Robertson, A S 2000 *An Inventory of Romano-British Coin Hoards*. London: Royal Numismatic Society.

Ross, A 1974 'A pagan Celtic tricephalos from Netherton, Lanarkshire', *Glasgow Archaeol J* 3, 26-33.

Ross, A 1994 'Pottery report', in Ballin Smith 1994, 236-256.

Roymans, N 2004 *Ethnic identity and imperial power: the Batavians in the early Roman empire*. Amsterdam: Amsterdam University Press.

Sekulla, M F 1982 'The Roman coins from Traprain Law', *Proc Soc Antiq Scot* 112, 285-294.

Sharples, N 2003 'From monuments to artefacts: changing social relationships in the later Iron Age', in J Downes & A Ritchie (ed), *Sea Change: Orkney and Northern Europe in the later Iron Age AD 300-800*, 151-165. Balgavies: Pinkfoot Press.

Shepherd, I A G 1983 'Pictish settlement problems in N.E. Scotland', in J C Chapman & H C Mytum (ed), *Settlement in North Britain 1000 BC – AD 1000*, 327-356. Oxford: BAR.

Shepherd, I A G 1993 'The Picts in Moray', in W D H Sellar (ed), *Moray: Province and People*, 75-90. Edinburgh: Scottish Society for Northern Studies.

Sibbald, R 1707 *Historical Inquiries concerning Roman monuments and antiquities in the north part of Britain called Scotland*. Edinburgh: James Watson.

Small, A 1987 *The Picts: a new look at old problems*. Dundee: Graham Hunter Foundation.

Smith, I M 1991 'Sprouston, Roxburghshire: an early Anglian centre of the eastern Tweed basin', *Proc Soc Antiq Scot* 121, 261-294.

Smith, J 1919 'Excavation of the forts of Castlehill, Aitnock, and Coalhill, Ayrshire', *Proc Soc Antiq Scot* 53 (1918-19), 123-134.

Smyth, A P 1989 *Warlords and Holy Men: Scotland AD 80-1000*. Edinburgh: EUP.

Snape, M E 1993 *Roman brooches from North Britain: a classification and a catalogue of brooches from sites on the Stanegate*. Oxford: BAR.

Spearman, R M 1990 'The Helmsdale bowls, a re-assessment', *Proc Soc Antiq Scot* 120, 63-77.

Spearman, R M & Higgitt, J (ed) 1993 *The age of migrating ideas*. Edinburgh: NMS.

Stead, I M 1967 'A La Tène III burial at Welwyn Garden City', *Archaeologia* 101, 1-62.

Stevenson, J B 1993 'Cup-and-ring markings at Ballochmyle, Ayrshire', *Glasgow Archaeol J* 18, 33-40.

Stevenson, R B K 1956a 'Native bangles and Roman glass', *Proc Soc Antiq Scot* 88 (1954-6), 208-221.

Stevenson, R B K 1956b 'Pictish chain, Roman silver and bauxite beads', *Proc Soc Antiq Scot* 88 (1954-6), 228-230.

Stoklund, M 2003 'The first runes – the literary language of the Germani', in Jørgensen et al 2003, 172-179.

Tait, H (ed) 1976 *Jewellery through 7000 years*. London: British Museum.

Thomas, C 1961 'The animal art of the Scottish Iron Age and its origins', *Archaeol J* 118, 14-64.

Thomas, C 1994 *And shall these mute stones speak? Post-Roman inscriptions in western Britain*. Cardiff: University of Wales Press.

Tipping, R 1994 'The form and fate of Scotland's woodlands', *Proc Soc Antiq Scot* 124, 1-54.

Tipping, R 1997 'Pollen analysis and the impact of Rome on native agriculture around Hadrian's Wall', in Gwilt & Haselgrove 1997, 239-247.

Todd, M 1985 'The Falkirk hoard of denarii: trade or subsidy?', *Proc Soc Antiq Scot* 115, 229-232.

Turner, V, Dockrill, S, Bond, J, Batt, C & Brown, L 2002 'Old Scatness and the broch lairds of the north', *Current Archaeology* 177, 382-390.

Tyers, P 1996 *Roman Pottery in Britain*. London: Routledge.

Voß, H-U 1998 *Corpus der römischen Funde im europäischen Barbaricum. Deutschland Band 3:Bundesland Mecklenburg-Vorpommern*. Bonn: Rudolf Habelt.

Wainwright, F T 1953 'A souterrain identified in Angus', *Antiq J* 33, 65-71.

Wainwright, F T 1956 'The Picts and the problem', in F T Wainwright (ed), *The Problem of the Picts*, 1-53. Edinburgh: Thomas Nelson.

Wainwright, F T 1963 *The souterrains of southern Pictland*. London: Routledge & Kegan Paul.

Wallace, C 2006 'Long-lived Samian?', *Britannia* 37, 259-272.

Warner, R B 1976 'Some observations on the context and importation of exotic material in Ireland, from the first century BC to the second century AD', *Proc Royal Irish Academy* 76C, 267-292.

Watkins, T 1984 'Where were the Picts? An essay in settlement archaeology', in Friell & Watson (ed), 63-86.

Watson, W J 1926 *The history of the Celtic placenames of Scotland*. Edinburgh: Blackwood.

Webster, J 2003 'Art as resistance and negotiation', in S Scott & J Webster (ed), *Roman imperialism and provincial art*, 24-51. Cambridge: CUP.

Wells, P S 1999 *The barbarians speak: how the conquered peoples shaped Roman Europe*. Princeton: Princeton University Press.

Wheeler, R E M 1935 *London and the Saxons*. London: London Museum (Catalogue 6).

Wheeler, M 1954 *The Stanwick fortifications, North Riding of Yorkshire*. Oxford: Society of Antiquaries of London.

Whittington, G & Edwards, K J 1993 '*Ubi solitudinem faciunt pacem appellant*: the Romans in Scotland, a palaeoenvironmental contribution', *Britannia* 24, 13-25.

Willis, S 1997 'Samian: beyond dating', in K Meadows, C Lemke & J Heron (ed) *TRAC 96: Proceedings of the Sixth Annual Theoretical Roman Archaeology Conference Sheffield 1996*, 38-54. Oxford: Oxbow.

Willis, S 1998a 'Iron Age and Roman pottery', in Main 1998, 321-331.

Willis, S 1998b 'Samian pottery in Britain: exploring its distribution and archaeological potential', *Archaeol J* 155, 82-133.

Wilson, A 2001 'The Novantae and Romanization in Galloway', *Trans Dumfries Galloway Nat Hist Antiq Soc* 75, 73-131.

Wilson, A 2003 'Roman and native in Dumfriesshire', *Trans Dumfries Galloway Nat Hist Antiq Soc* 77, 103-160.

Wilson, E M 1980 'Excavations at West Mains of Ethie, Angus', *Proc Soc Antiq Scot* 110 (1978-80), 114-121.

Woolf, A 1998 'Romancing the Celts: a segmentary approach to acculturation', in R Laurence & J Berry (ed), *Cultural Identity in the Roman Empire*, 111-124. London: Routledge.

Younger, H J 1936 'Excavation of a kitchen-midden near Gullane', *Proc Soc Antiq Scot* 70 (1935-6), 332-341.

Zwierlein-Diehl, E 1998 *Der Dreikönigenschrein im Kölner Dom 1: Die Gemmen und Kameen des Dreikönigenschreines*. Köln: Verlag Kölner Dom.

Notes

[1] For sources and discussion see Rivet & Smith 1979, 289-291; Breeze 1997; Fraser 2005, 33-37; Hind 1983; Mann & Breeze 1987; Barrow 1989; Watson 1926, 20-21; Richmond 1961.

[2] The name is restored from the original *Anavion[ens](ium)*, with letters in square brackets a restoration of damage and those in round brackets an expansion of epigraphic abbreviations.

[3] Alcock 1963; Alcock & Alcock 1987, 131; *ibid* 1990, 115-116. See also for Ireland Warner 1976, 285-288; Bélier 1982; Bradley 1982; and, for a useful discussion of material from the north Netherlands, Galestin 1999 and Erdrich 1999.

[4] This develops an idea noted in the Early Historic period with penannular brooches (Nieke 1993, 130).

[5] Exceptions are rare, but note the small bronze cups from Lamberton Moor, Berwickshire, and a ceramic skeuomorph from Howe, Orkney; also a small wooden cup from Dervaird Moss, Wigtownshire (MacGregor 1976, nos 292-6; Ross 1994, 248, no 7114, illus 147-148; Maxwell 1951, fig 4.3; Earwood 1989, 64-67, 272 (recorded as Dalvaird, which seems to be a mis-representation of Dervaird)).

[6] Except for Traprain (Erdrich et al 2000), which in many ways is atypical of the general picture.

[7] A possible exception to this, which I overlooked in earlier work, is Burnswark in Dumfriesshire. The sequence on this hillfort and its relation to Roman incursions has been hotly debated, but the range of Roman Iron Age finds recovered from Jobey's relatively limited investigations points to a rich native site with extensive access to Roman material (Jobey 1978; Wilson 2003, 131-136). The rest of the region lacks evidence of such focal sites (Wilson 2001).

[8] Simple Nauheim-derivative brooches are treated as ERIA since, although their origins undoubtedly lie earlier, they appear on Flavian sites such as Newstead and Elginhaugh and thus could be contemporary with the initial conquest (Curle 1911, 318; Hanson forthcoming). This is supported by the number of such brooches known from the Stanegate frontier (Snape 1993, 97-100). Scottish examples come from Luce Sands, Wigtownshire and an unknown site in Dumfriesshire (NMS unpub; Robertson 1970, 222). There is also an example from Norwick, Unst, Shetland (Cambridge & Watt 2003) which is an unusual form, potentially pre-Roman. Although outwith the geographical scope of the current work, it is worth noting the Hod Hill brooch and another unusual early bow brooch from Dod Law West, Northumberland (Allason-Jones 1989).

[9] The late Roman pottery is currently under study by Colin Wallace.

[10] To take the latter as an example, only six of the 140 or so brooches known from non-Roman sites in Scotland are late Roman types, while data from northern England suggest a proportion of 152 out of 526 bow brooches (almost 30%; Snape 1993, table 4).

[11] As suggested also by late Roman finds on southern Scottish fort sites (e.g.

Cramond: Hartley 2003, 57 no 16; Ford 2003, nos 175, 252-253); more generally see Robertson 1983, Table 2.

[12] Spearman's dating is unduly broad; the presence of an Irchester-type bowl (2 in his catalogue) confirms a late Roman date, most probably fourth century (Kennett 1968, 29-32; de Micheli 1992).

[13] See also Bradley 1982 for medieval references to use as a medicine. There is of course plentiful evidence for reuse of samian within the province; Cool (2000, 52-53) has noted preferential reuse of samian as spindle whorls in the late Roman period.

[14] Significant additions since this survey are deer carvings from Ballochmyle, Ayrshire (Stevenson 1993, 38-9); Blackford Hill, Midlothian (DES 2005, 62); and, most strikingly, the deer and horses from Eggerness, Wigtownshire (Morris & van Hoek 1987).

[15] Defined in Ashmore's terms as those with a date weakness of less than 20; methodology follows that in Ashmore 2004. The analysis included dates known as of April 2003.

[16] The areas were based on grid squares, as this was the easiest system for analysis. This obviously over-runs geographical divisions so that, for instance, the western area includes parts of the western Atlantic region. However, for a preliminary study this was considered adequate.

[17] The map is slightly misleading, as it gives the impression of pan-British types. In fact these are unsurprising finds in northern contexts but unexpected ones found in very low proportions in southern assemblages.

[18] The apparent concentration in 'southern Pictland' is an artificial feature caused by the dominance of aerial photographic evidence in this area; recent survey in Strathdon by RCAHMS has shown that, when biases in the data are taken into account, such souterrains are common right across the north-east (Strat Halliday, pers comm).

[19] Although of course architectural display need not focus on defences, as archaeologists tend to; we know nothing of differences in the appearance of buildings above ground level.

[20] See assorted papers in *Tayside & Fife Archaeol J* 9 and 10 (2003-4) for the first fruits of this work.

[21] Excavations by CFA Archaeology revealed an area with bronze-casting evidence, associated radiocarbon dates suggesting a third-fifth century AD date. Post-excavation work is ongoing, but there is so far no indication of any previous Iron Age activity (information courtesy of Ian Suddaby).

[22] Rendered by Cessford (1997, fig 7) as a series of spiral scrolls, but from the replica in NMS it is more like a pelta with spiral terminals.

[23] A slightly more detailed provenance is given in Sibbald (1707) on an unnumbered plate: 'Fibula argentea found near the River Forth and not far from the Wall'. It is also illustrated, without a caption, in Gordon (1726, plate IV no 9). I am grateful to Lawrence Keppie for the Sibbald reference.